WORLD PERSPECTIVES

———— 7 ————

Man and Materialism

WORLD PERSPECTIVES

Planned and Edited by Ruth Nanda Anshen

Jacques Maritain: *Approaches to God*
Walter Gropius: *Scope of Total Architecture*
Radhakrishnan: *Recovery of Faith*
Brock Chisholm: *Can Nations Learn to Learn?*
Lewis Mumford: *The Transformations of Man*
Konrad Adenauer: *World Indivisible*
V. G. Childe: *Society and Knowledge*
Fred Hoyle: *Man and Materialism*
Erich Fromm: *The Art of Loving*
Paul Tillich: *Dynamics of Faith*
D. T. Suzuki: *Mysticism*
Denis de Rougemont: *Man's Western Quest*
Edmund W. Sinnott: *Matter, Mind and Man*
Martin C. D'Arcy: *The Meeting of Love and Knowledge*
W. Heisenberg: *Physics and Philosophy*
Sivami Nikhilanandu: *Hinduism*
Erich Fromm: *Sigmund Freud's Mission*

WORLD PERSPECTIVES

FRED HOYLE

Man and Materialism

GEORGE ALLEN & UNWIN LTD
RUSKIN HOUSE
MUSEUM STREET LONDON

First Published in Great Britain in 1957
Second Impression 1959

Printed in Great Britain by
Butler & Tanner Ltd, Frome

WORLD PERSPECTIVES

What this Series Means

WORLD PERSPECTIVES is a plan to present short books in a variety of fields by the most responsible of contemporary thinkers. The purpose is to reveal basic new trends in modern civilization, to interpret the creative forces at work in the East as well as in the West, and to point to the new consciousness which can contribute to a deeper understanding of the inter-relation of man and the universe, the individual and society, and of the values shared by all people. WORLD PERSPECTIVES represents the world community of ideas in a universe of discourse, emphasising the principle of unity in mankind, of permanence within change.

Recent developments in many fields of thought have opened unsuspected prospects for a deeper understanding of man's situation and for a proper appreciation of human values and human aspirations. These prospects, though the outcome of purely specialized studies in limited fields, require for their analysis and synthesis a new structure and frame in which they can be explored, enriched and advanced in all their aspects for the benefit of man and society. Such a structure and frame it is the endeavour of WORLD PERSPECTIVES to define leading hopefully to a doctrine of man.

A further purpose of this Series is to attempt to overcome a principal ailment of humanity, namely, the effects of the atomization of knowledge produced by the overwhelming accretion of facts which science has created ; to clarify and synthesise ideas through the *depth* fertilization of minds ; to show from diverse and important points of view the correlation of ideas, facts and values which are in perpetual interplay ; to

v

demonstrate the character, kinship, logic and operation of the entire organism of reality while showing the persistent inter-relationship of the processes of the human mind and in the interstices of knowledge, to reveal the inner synthesis and organic unity of life itself.

It is the thesis of WORLD PERSPECTIVES that in spite of the difference and diversity of the disciplines represented, there exists a strong common agreement among its authors concerning the overwhelming need for counterbalancing the multitude of compelling scientific activities and investigations of objective phenomena from physics to metaphysics, history and biology and to relate these to meaningful experience. To provide this balance, it is necessary to stimulate an awareness of the basic fact that ultimately the individual human personality must tie all the loose ends together into an organic whole, must relate himself to himself, to mankind and society while deepening and enhancing his communion with the universe. To anchor this spirit and to impress it on the intellectual and spiritual life of humanity, on thinkers and doers alike, is indeed an enormous challenge and cannot be left entirely either to natural science on the one hand or to organized religion on the other. For we are confronted with the unbending necessity to discover a principle of differentiation yet relatedness lucid enough to justify and purify scientific, philosophic and all other know-ledge while accepting their mutual interdependence. This is the crisis in consciousness made articulate through the crisis in science. This is the new awakening.

This Series is committed to the recognition that all great changes are preceded by a vigorous intellectual re-evaluation and reorganization. Our authors are aware that the sin of hubris may be avoided by showing that the creative process itself is not a free activity if by free we mean arbitrary or unrelated to cosmic law. For the creative process in the human mind, the developmental process in organic nature and the basic laws of the inorganic realm may be but varied expressions of a universal formative process. Thus WORLD PERSPECTIVES hopes to show that although the present apocalyptic period is one of exceptional tensions, there is also an exceptional movement at work towards a compensating unity which cannot violate the ultimate moral power pervading the universe, that very power on which all human effort must at last depend. In this way, we may come to understand that there exists an independence of spiritual and mental growth which though conditioned by circumstances is never determined by circumstances. In this way the great plethora of human knowledge may be correlated with an insight into the nature of human nature by being attuned to the wide and deep range of human thought and human experience. For what is lacking is not the knowledge of the structure of the universe but a consciousness of the qualitative uniqueness of human life.

And finally, it is the thesis of this Series that man is in the process of developing a new awareness which, in spite of his apparent spiritual and moral captivity, can eventually lift the human race above and beyond the fear, ignorance, brutality and isolation which beset it to-day. It is to this nascent consciousness, to this concept of man born out of a fresh vision of reality, that WORLD PERSPECTIVES is dedicated.

NEW YORK, 1958.   RUTH NANDA ANSHEN

Contents

		PAGE
	PREAMBLE	ix
1	The Tangled Skein	3
2	The Tangible Aspects of Communism	8
3	The Intangible Aspects	19
4	The Historical Record	25
5	The Significance of Industrialism	51
6	The Thing	65
7	A Biological Paradox Resolved	75
8	What is the Mind ?	82
9	The Relationship of Individual and Community	94
10	The Evolution of Humanity	113
11	Crisis in the Modern World : The First Problem	118
12	Population : The Second Problem	122
13	Fossilization : The Third Problem	141
14	The Religious Impulse in Man	150

Preamble

WHAT is a materialist? In the popular view I suppose a materialist is a pretty unpleasant person who gobbles babies for breakfast. This is a view I do not agree with. I am a materialist and I haven't gobbled any babies, yet.

Nor has materialism anything to do with Soviet Communism. It is true that Communists profess a crude style of materialism, but this has small similarity with the deeper materialism of the Western world.

The essence of materialism lies in a refusal to separate Man and his environment into the mutually exclusive categories of "spiritual" and "material." Man is regarded as belonging to the Universe, not necessarily insignificantly, as a star or a galaxy belongs to the Universe. Star, galaxy, man, are all expressions of the structure of the Universe. No attempt is made to introduce the notions of value or importance. A star is not necessarily more important than a man, or vice versa. Star and man are in the same boat (if the phrase be permitted); they are both expressions of the same inner laws. This point of view lies at the base of the present book, although it enters explicitly only in the final chapter.

It is urged by the opponents of materialism that while it has been found possible to understand in some detail how stars behave, no one has so far been able to understand with real precision how men behave. Instead of admitting this as proof that stars and men belong to rootedly different categories, the materialist points out that a star is a much simpler structure than a man, so it is no wonder that we know more about the inside of a star than we know about the inside of our own heads. The materialist cannot remain content with this, however. He will only score a complete victory over his opponents if he is able to show that the behavior of Man can indeed be understood with precision, thereby destroying the case against him.

The present volume contains my own attempt on this problem. Let me say at once that I shall be surprised if the reader finds the attempt wholly successful; the problems are too difficult for any writer to hold more than partial success as an ambition. Now why is the problem so difficult? In mathematical terms, because human behavior is controlled by an interlocking system of nonlinear feedback loops. A word of explanation is needed.

Consider an investor buying and selling shares on the Stock Exchange. So long as the number of shares involved is not too large our investor's activities are "linear." That is to say, the sums of money concerned in purchases and sales are in simple proportion to the numbers of shares that are bought and sold. But this is not so if the number of shares is very large. The selling or buying in this case disturbs the market itself, and the sums of money are not in direct proportion to the numbers of shares involved. The investor's activities now possess "feedback"; his financial dealings are no longer linear.

It is far beyond present-day resources to take full and accurate account of all the feedback effects that occur in human society. Every sociological, economic, or political discussion must of necessity be an oversimplification of the complete problem. A crucial question always arises whenever a conclusion is reached in such discussions: "Would the same conclusion have been reached if there had been no oversimplification?"

Evidently no conclusion is of any value unless the answer to this question is affirmative—indeed if the answer is not affirmative the conclusion is pernicious nonsense! But in the absence of a nonsimplified solution how can we know whether the answer is affirmative or not? Herein lies the dilemma of all social studies.

Although the dilemma is very awkward, a complete pessimism is not justified. Conclusions can, for instance, be subjected to the acid test of experience. This would be a sovereign receipt if testing by experience were always possible—but a government cannot delay a decision on foreign policy until after the events with which the policy is concerned are over and done with! This circumstance frequently leads to the use of an empirical analogy, the logic being this:

1. Present conditions are similar to the conditions that occurred on a certain occasion in the past.
2. Such-and-such an outcome actually occurred in the former case.
3. The same outcome will follow in the present case.

No mathematician will need warning of the dangers in this argument. Past and present conditions are never exactly identical, and even very small differences can (the problem being nonlinear) cause severe divergences in the outcome.* This I believe to be the cause of the frequent mistakes made by politicians the world over—and indeed by all who are concerned in any way with predicting the course of human events. Predicting by analogy contains many pitfalls.

The next possibility lies in limiting the scope of our inquiry. Suppose we consider only the fate of groups of men, not of individuals. Then simplifications may be expected, in much the way that problems in physics become comparatively simple when statistical averaging over a large number of particles can be introduced. We must not be too greedy in our studies or too egocentric. To begin with at any rate, we must limit ourselves to human communities in the large and must eschew the what-is-going-to-happen-to-me mentality.

We can gain further statistical simplicity, as Sir Charles Darwin has pointed out in *The Next Million Years*,† if we content ourselves with long-term trends, if we do not attempt to predict day-by-day changes or even year-by-year changes in human society. There is indeed some reason to believe that short-term changes usually arise from chance fluctuations ("noise" to the physicist) and are inherently unpredictable.

Here then is the general method followed in the present book. We shall be concerned with communities in the large, we shall be concerned only with long-term trends (the century being a typical time scale), and we shall employ empirical tests whenever possible. The historical record is very important

* The flight of a golf ball has "feedback" and is nonlinear, especially on a windy day, when very slight difference in making a shot can produce enormous differences in the outcome!

† Doubleday, New York, 1952.

in this connection. History, once the chance fluctuations referred to above have been stripped out of it, is a veritable storehouse of empirical evidence concerning human behavior. No discussion of Man can be attempted without history. Hence the account in Chapter IV.

Following this plan, we find that some of the matters that in our day-to-day life we regard as of great importance become relegated to insignificance compared with other problems of long-term urgency. The layout of the book is this:

Chapters I–III   Day-to-day problems whose importance is probably much exaggerated.

Chapter IV   The historical record.

Chapters V–X   The detailed arguments for my conclusions.

Chapters XI–XIV   The problems that I believe to be of long-term importance.

The reader will not find any single simple thread in chapters V–X. Rather does the discussion range widely afield as indeed it must if the interlocking factors that control human destiny are to be at all understood. Man's evolution is a compound of many threads. Any argument that sought to reduce it to a single strand would be too gross an oversimplification.

FRED HOYLE

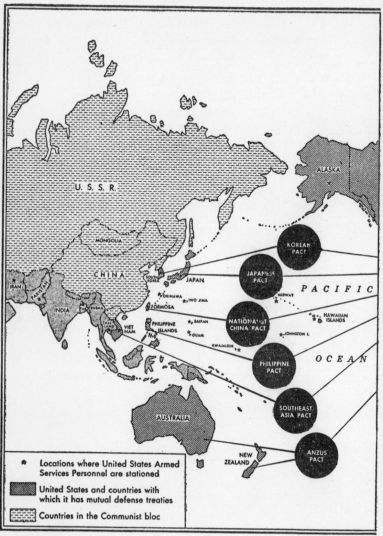

FIGURE 1

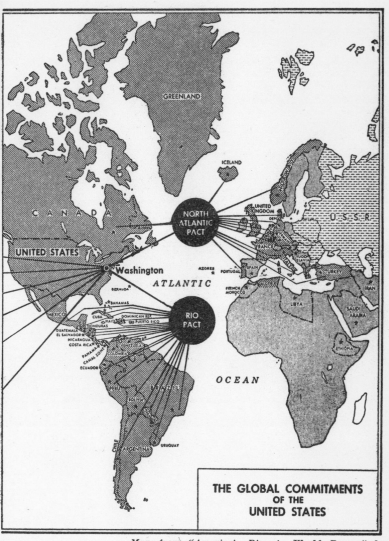

GREENLAND

ICELAND

CANADA

NORTH
ATLANTIC
PACT

UNITED KINGDOM

DEN.

U.S.S.R.

UNITED STATES

★ Washington

AZORES ★

FRANCE

YUGO-
SLAVIA

TURKEY

IRAN

ATLANTIC

PORTUGAL

SPAIN

FRENCH
MOROCCO

ALGERIA

BERMUDA

MEXICO

BAHAMAS

CUBA

HAITI

DOMINICAN REP.

PUERTO RICO

GUATEMALA

HONDURAS

EL SALVADOR

NICARAGUA

COSTA RICA

PANAMA

CANAL ZONE

ECUADOR

VENEZUELA

COLOMBIA

RIO
PACT

LIBYA

SAUDI
ARABIA

ETHIOPIA

OCEAN

PERU

BRAZIL

BOLIVIA

CHILE

ARGENTINA

URUGUAY

**THE GLOBAL COMMITMENTS
OF THE
UNITED STATES**

*Map from "America's Rise to World Power," by
Foster Rhea Dulles, used by permission of the author*

I.

The Tangled Skein

MUCH of humanity today fights under one or other of two banners, of Communism and Anti-Communism. The banners have become symbols that stand for many things, for so many things that by now no one quite knows what. When those of us who fight under the banner of Anti-Communism are asked to explain why we fight thus, in our ignorance we are forced to answer, "Because the men who support Communism are evil," and those who are regarded as the staunchest fighters for Anti-Communism would add, "And that is good enough for me." I don't know whether fighters for the banner of Communism justify themselves by a similar argument but I suspect that they do.

When I was a boy I often fought under a banner. The boys of our village would fight the boys of another village because they had invaded our "bird-nesting" territory, because they had "pinched" a dog belonging to one of our lads, or even for no other reason than that they were boys of another village. We would meet in Homeric battle in some farmer's field. With a continuous whooping and roaring, one band of boys would

3   B

close in combat with the other. There would then come such a punching and pummeling as used to delight the eyes of adult passers-by. Strange to say, these little affairs seemed to do everybody good—with the exception of a few who came off with what Shakespeare would have called a bloody cox-comb; and even these had completely recovered by the morrow and were able to parade themselves as heroes for the rest of the week.

If a world war were no more serious in its impact than a battle between two herds of boys we should have little to worry about. But everyone knows that this is not so. Forty million people met their deaths in the last world war and powers of destruction have increased enormously since then. I think that few would disagree with the opinion that another world war might easily lead to a hundred million deaths, and that none of the participating peoples would escape from mak-ing a due contribution to the grisly total.

By a curious irony an appreciation of this terrible situation has become common ground to both Communists and Anti-Communists. Neither wishes to bring about the destruction of vast numbers of innocent people, counting many children among them. Neither wishes to court the downfall of civiliza-tion. Yet what other recourse is possible? When humanity divides itself into two camps, when each camp assembles itself beneath its own particular banner, when each brandishes its fist unceasingly at the other, how can such a conflict be re-solved except by total war?

These are questions that I think each one of us should attempt to answer for himself. For my own part, I do not know whether there is any possibility of avoiding a disastrous holocaust, and I doubt whether anyone can give a certainly correct opinion on this. But of one thing I do feel certain: that the banner mentality does not improve our chances of averting disaster. Rather should we try to understand what the symbols on the banners mean. It is not enough to say that Communism is evil; we must try to understand as best we can exactly what Communism is, and why we are opposed to it. Only so shall we come to know where the snares lie along the path that we must follow.

Unfortunately an exposition of the nature of Communism is a matter of extraordinary difficulty. This is because the concept of Communism is now woven out of many threads: the police state, espionage, the suppression of the individual, the strength of Russian armaments, the increasing meaninglessness of life, the nature of private and public enterprise in general, social medicine, the retreat of the old religious views, anti-colonialism among native peoples. All these and others as well are components in our concept of what we mean by Communism.

Some people may object to this anatomizing on the grounds that they themselves do not understand certain of these items as being components of the communist issue. This may well be the case because those of us who are mustered under the Anti-Communist banner are very far from being agreed on what it is that we are against. Therein lies one of our most serious difficulties.

It is easy to see how this situation has come about. For the last thirty years the word "communist" has been a term of general opprobrium in the West. This has led us to associate many of the things that we dislike most with Communism and with the communists. In this way our ideas have acquired accretions that have changed the concept of Communism from what it used to be. There is little to connect the Communism of the present day with the Paris Commune of eighty years ago.

This process of increasing damnation has turned out to have very serious disadvantages. Quite apart from the truism that it is not always an advantage to paint one's opponents blacker than they really are, a wholly unnecessary degree of confusion has been caused thereby within the Anti-Communist camp. We are paying bitterly for this confusion at the present time. During the last two or three years there has been the danger of a rift opening up between the United States and the British Commonwealth. This danger arises from the different ways that "Communism" has been colored in Britain and in the United States. By now the British understand by "Communism" something appreciably different from what the people of the United States do. It is this difference that has led the British not only to recognize the communist government of China, but to be astonished that the United States does not do likewise.

I hope enough has been said for the point I wish to make in this chapter to be considered as now established: that our first duty if we are to discuss Communism (and we can scarcely say very much about world affairs without bringing Communism into the discussion) is to ask what Communism is. I am sure that if we can agree on an answer to this question, however complicated the answer may be, we shall find that quite a number of our present difficulties either disappear altogether or will be comparatively simple of solution.

But the next step is an awkward one. By now the whole matter has become so complicated and so charged with emotion that it would surely take a visitor from another planet to consider it with a proper impartiality. The attempt is not to be avoided however.

II.

The Tangible Aspects of Communism

LET ME begin with the aspects of Communism to which I object most strongly myself. I object to the police state, with its constant spying and its torture chambers. I object to the raids of the goon squads by night and the dispensing of political justice by day. I object to all those features that aim to reduce the individual to a cog in the state machine. This is an issue over which I would be prepared to fight, for I do not consider my life to weigh so heavily as the rights of the individual as they are understood in the West. I would go even further: if I thought the reduction of humanity to an ant-like existence inevitable, then, quite frankly, I would have little interest left in the survival of the human species. I would feel that the sooner we got ourselves out of the way and left the road open for the evolution of some other animal of nobler aspirations the better.

Yet with this said, one must agree that the police state is not unique to the communists, nor is it even of their invention. Belsen, Dachau, the gas chambers of the Gestapo are still too fresh in our memories for us to make any mistake on this.

Rather does it seem as if wave after wave of mass brutality—brutishness might perhaps be a better word—has swept over the world in the last few decades. Communism represents but one of these waves. This being so, we must I think be on our guard against supposing that the defeat of Communism will necessarily solve all our problems, any more than the defeat of the Hitlerites solved all the world's problems. I suspect that the present sickness of the human race lies somewhat deeper than the struggle against Communism, important as this is.

Another conclusion that I believe to be valid is that brutishness cannot be successfully combated by brutishness. It is this that makes me doubt whether a war launched to defeat Communism will succeed in its broader aims. To defeat Communism in a way that caused the deaths of tens of millions of women and children would not I think persuade the world that salvation had been worth while. Herein lies one of the peculiar difficulties of the situation. We are in a position where real victory can only be achieved by persuasion and example, not by a deliberate display of force. This does not mean that we should not be fortified to defend ourselves in case of an out-and-out physical assault by the communists; of course we should.

Persuasion demands that we should scrupulously avoid adopting any of the noxious political practices of the communists. This is so manifestly clear that I am the more surprised that many who proclaim themselves publicly to be the strongest opponents of Communism seem quite ready, and even anxious, to adopt methods that are strikingly similar to those of the communists themselves. Bluntly expressed, these individuals give the impression of wanting to substitute the policeman's dossier in place of the Constitution and the Bill of Rights. If they should succeed, the communists will indeed have gone far toward securing a final victory; for the world is not I think interested in making a choice between one tyranny and another but only in a choice between tyranny and freedom.

Let us pass now to the second of the three topics to be considered in the present chapter, to the military threat of Russia. The debit and credit sides of the balance sheet can here be summarized quickly. On the debit side, Russia undoubtedly possesses an army of great numerical strength and, judging by its performance in the late war, of great striking power too. Of an equal seriousness in my opinion is the rapid advance of Russian technology. In the development of jet aircraft and of the atomic bomb, Russia gave the impression of hanging on a good way behind the West, but the communists were not a long way behind with the hydrogen bomb—unfortunately they were very nearly in the lead, a situation that would have seemed well-nigh impossible ten years ago. I very much fear that we must admit that Russian technology is now going ahead at as least as fast a rate as Western technology.

Let us turn now to the positive side of the picture. First we may take stock of the reassuring situation shown in Figure 1, which gives the locations throughout the world of the military bases operated by the Western Powers. Add to this strategic position the undoubtedly far greater industrial capacity of the West and it is clear that our case is being backed up by a real show of strength. In thus surrounding communist territory by military bases our leaders have evidently done a thoroughly good job: there is no question of a softness toward Communism here.

But this balance-sheet accounting does not give a complete view of the strategy of world affairs. A new factor, different from any previous balance-of-power struggle, has invaded the present situation; for both sides now possess sufficient strength to do mortal hurt to the other—this being the considered opinion of the great majority of those who have studied the destructive power of nuclear weapons. War is no longer a simple means of settling nationalistic rivalries, as it was in the First World War. Nor is it a means of ridding the world of a detestable state of affairs, as it was in the Second World War. The most that we can now gain from war is the total destruction of our opponents, knowing that in the process we ourselves will also irrevocably be destroyed. War is now synonymous with suicide.

This being I believe an undoubtedly correct assessment, I am at a loss I must confess to understand the full implications of the strategy illustrated by Figure 1, a strategy that looks very much like an old-fashioned policy of containment. The idea of a containment policy is: first to decide on a line drawn over the Earth's surface, then to announce that a step across the line by the opposing side will be taken as equivalent to an open declaration of war. In former times this procedure had considerable merit to recommend it. With the position of the line stated, both sides knew exactly where they were; the consequences of a fateful step across were clearly understood.

So the chance of war starting through a misunderstanding was thereby reduced to a minimum. Indeed many wars have probably been averted altogether by this policy.

For containment to work satisfactorily, the side that elects to draw the line must mean strict business. There must be no suspicion of a bluff. Otherwise an aggressive move may be made by one side in the belief that the other will back down in a pinch. If the other side does not then back down, war breaks out in earnest, even though no one may really have wanted it. The First World War started in much this way, Germany being uncertain as to whether Britain would declare war in the event of a German attack on the Channel ports. The German decision that Britain would not declare war turned out to be wrong—with the result that modern civilization was overtaken by its first major disaster.

Even before the atomic age, the satisfactory operation of a containment policy demanded steady nerves and cool judgment; and sometimes nerves and judgment failed, as German and British nerves and judgment failed in 1914. The difficulties inherent in containment are much more severe today. Consider the world-wide span of the line that joins our defensive bases, the bases shown in Figure 1. Are we really going to start a world war if this line is crossed at any place? Are we going to invite complete self-destruction? Are we going to endanger the whole fabric of civilization? Or are we going to back down? Are we just bluffing?

The dilemma of the containment policy is obvious. If we bluff then we run the danger that the communists will encroach more and more across the line. If we do not bluff then we court entire disaster, the only satisfaction being that we can bring the communists down in a ruin equal to our own—or perhaps worse than our own, if that should be any satisfaction.

There is a further, very serious complicating factor. The struggle is not between two coherent opposing forces. The late war in Indo-China for instance was not a straight issue between Washington and Moscow, or between Washington and Peking. In this particular case, mixed in with the political aspects of Communism was an anticolonial sentiment, a hatred of domination by the white man, a hatred that has become a strong force in Asia during the last few decades. The aim of the Viet-Minh army was as much to throw the French out of Indo-China as it was to support the schemes of Moscow.

The fact that neither the Communists nor the Anti-Communists fit into clearly defined categories, the fact that each is a highly complex association of many different peoples, the fact that the issues that seem of main importance in Indo-China are not the same as those in Germany make a policy of containment extraordinarily difficult to operate. When the communists cross the line, how can we be sure that the action is due to the deep-laid schemes of Moscow, and not to some local partisan issue? And unless we are sure of this, how can we take the risk of plunging the world into a nuclear war, a war that may bring down our whole civilization?

Yet if we cannot operate a containment policy how can we prevent ourselves from being nibbled to death (to use a politicism) by communist encroachment? How can we prevent the marxist forces on the other side of the line from spreading all over the world?

These remarks bring out the well-nigh contradictory character of present-day strategy. I get the impression that present policy is a makeshift that has arisen out of the policies of former generations. These did not work very well even in their own day (as in the outbreak of the First World War), and are likely to work less well under future conditions. It seems to me that although neither the Communists nor the Anti-Communists want to find themselves in a nuclear war, the policies now being followed (on both sides) make it very possible that a nuclear war will in fact occur.

I am not able to put forward any patent receipt. The only opinion I would offer here is that a less rigid outlook on both sides would probably be helpful.

With an apology for this pessimistic view, I would like now to take up the last of the three topics of this chapter; namely the difference of economic outlook between Communists and Anti-Communists, between Communism and Capitalism, that is to say.

As a first step it may be said that Communism and Capitalism are rather like the negative and positive of the same photograph. In capitalistic society the great bulk of property and industry is owned by individuals and the "State" is supported by taxes raised on private companies and on individuals. In communistic society things are just the other way round; effectively all property and industry is owned by the "State," individuals being rewarded for their work at the pleasure of the "State."

There is nothing in this to provide an immediately sensible

reason why two societies adopting such opposite social organizations should be at each other's throats; any more than there was a sensible reason why Swift's Lilliputians should have risen in revolt against the practice of Littlendianism. Even when we look further into the matter it does not become easy to detect a sound reason for hostility. This will I hope become plain in the following discussion.

There are appreciable numbers of people living in capitalistic societies who express themselves as favoring the communistic type of organization. They say that Capitalism is "unfair," that it sustains the so-called privileged classes. This is certainly true. In an economic free-for-all, which is what Capitalism amounts to, it is certain that some individuals will come out of the mix-up better than others. Special abilities may play a part but even without differences of ability, chance fluctuations would eventually lead to some people becoming much wealthier than the average. According to the people who favor Communism there is something immoral about this inequality.

Now does the communistic form of society really provide equality for all? Of course it does not. This we can see by inquiring into the so-far undefined concept of "State." What is the "State"? In one sense it is the whole mass of a people and in another sense it is no more than the individuals who happen to form the governing group. In the present discussion it is the second interpretation that is of interest. The persons who govern, control all property in a communistic state. Do these people also take an equal share? Naturally they do not. They are the equivalent of the privileged class in capitalistic society. Indeed, a leader in a communist society is far more privileged than any capitalist could ever be. A capitalist at most controls only a fraction of an industry—the influence of even a Rocke-feller is limited—but a small group of communist leaders con-trol everything. They possess the whole of industry and they possess the physical power to dictate to the people what level of reward they must work for. No capitalist possesses any semblance of this latter power, hemmed in as he is by Trade Union activity. What it amounts to is this: in a capitalist society there is a large group of people possessing a limited degree of privilege. Whether a particular individual belongs to this group or not is largely a matter of chance. In a com-munistic society there is a perhaps smaller privileged class but what this class lacks in numbers it makes up in the very high degree of its privilege.

All this is so obvious as to make one wonder how anybody could be naïve enough to put forward the "fair share" argu-ment as a basis for favoring Communism. Actually not every-one using this argument really believes it. Those who do believe it usually describe themselves as Socialists, while those who use the argument but without believing in it are the communists. This is a distinction worth emphasizing at the expense of a diversion.

The communist living in a capitalist society advances the "fair share" argument because he thinks that by railing against the present privileged class he will persuade the bulk of people to favor a change-over to Communism. Should this happen he hopes to become a member of the fantastically privileged class that will rule the new state. Thus a communist is nearly always one who sees a change-over to Communism as a cheap way of obtaining what he covets. The communist is rather like a chess player who knocks over the board as soon as he finds that the game is lost.

Not all socialists are activated by such personal motives. Many socialists have themselves come from the privileged class. These have invariably been people who came to be obsessed with the moral implications of the "fair share" argument. Muddleheadedness underlies their statements and policies. Thus in the early days of Socialism it was believed that by taking over the possessions of the privileged classes and by distributing them equally all around the general standard of living could appreciably be raised. But the really privileged classes possess only a few per cent of the total wealth and hence even if the possessions of the wealthy were shared out equally there would be only a negligible change in the lot of the average man.

To come to more rational considerations, if the aim be a raising of the standard of living, the proper procedure should be to investigate the factors that control it, not to rush into crack-brained schemes. Now it is not at all difficult to see that the average standard of life is determined by dividing the productivity of a country by the number of its inhabitants. The society that manages to make this ratio largest will have the best standard of life, quite apart from how it elects to parcel out a few per cent of the total wealth among a privileged minority.

When this point was eventually dinned into British Socialists, they asserted, apparently giving little thought to the matter, that a communist form of state would yield the higher standard of productivity. This was an amazing assertion in view of the fact that the United States, organized on capitalistic lines, shows far and away the world's highest level of efficiency. It is true that special reasons can be put forward to explain this away, but the very fact that it is necessary to explain it away exposes the negligible grounds on which socialists make their assertions.

Although I think one must accept the view that the evidence on this issue is still inconclusive, it seems on psychological grounds that, other things being equal, Capitalism is likely to excel Communism in fertility of invention and in general productivity. Thus it is of the essence of Capitalism that those who employ inefficient methods do not tend to survive. It is true that examples can be found of restrictive practices, and of the refusal to put new discoveries into operation; but these cases are exceptions rather than the rule, and they occur precisely in very large concerns that possess practically a monopoly in a particular field. How much more would such practices occur when there was only one firm, namely the "State"? Not only this, but in a communist society those who control the "State" have as their prime concern, not the efficiency of industry, but the preservation of their own power. In a capitalist society, on the other hand, efficiency by and large comes first.

So we see nothing to show why a capitalist state should object to, and should be alarmed by, Communism as such. If anything, it would seem from what has just been said that the capitalist states ought to be congratulating themselves on possessing the better economic system, and ought to pity the others rather than be angry with them.

III.

The Intangible Aspects

THERE is a tendency to feel that one cannot easily point to all the objectionable features of Communism; that the discussion of the previous chapter leaves much unsaid; that indeed the more important things still remain unsaid. I think that many people feel the most dangerous element of Communism to be a sinister all-pervasive influence that no barrier seems capable of shutting out. Even when we contrive to set up a line of military defense, even when we succeed in preventing the official communist forces from crossing this line, it still seems as if communist subversion manages to infiltrate itself everywhere throughout our own territory.

The rather shadowy outline conjured up by these remarks needs marking in with more precision. How does communist infiltration show itself in actuality? The atomic spy rings spring immediately to mind. These were not ordinary cases of espionage. We usually think of a spy as a man who undertakes a dangerous job either for patriotic reasons or for the sordid reason of financial gain—this especially being the case with traitors. The outstanding atomic spies fit into neither of these

C

categories: their actions were prompted by reasons of ideology, of a preference for the doctrines of communism. When doctrines can thus cause an individual to betray his country, to betray secrets that might cause the deaths of millions of his fellow citizens, we must rightly regard them as both highly dangerous and most sinister.

Now how widespread are these cases of clear-cut defection? Respect for facts compels us to admit that the known cases of serious espionage are few in number. This is not to say that the known cases are unimportant, for each case in itself has involved matters of extreme gravity. But the number of severe cases is small. This cannot be denied. Yet a contrary general view is rather widespread. According to this view espionage is really taking place on a very large scale. The paucity of the number of proven cases is regarded as due to the incapacity of the FBI and of Congressional committees to break open the skillfully organized network of communist activity.

I do not myself believe this pessimistic opinion. A small group apart, it has seemed to me that the intellectual caliber of the communists who have figured in the spy trials has been rather low, so low that no large-scale organization that depended on such intelligence could possibly go undetected. I do not think that there is a scrap of evidence to show that the intensity of espionage is any greater today than it has been in the past, not only in the immediate past, but the past stretching back for a score of centuries or more—long before Communism was ever dreamed of. What is certainly true, however, is that a spy can be more dangerous today than spies ever were in the past.

The spate of investigations of the last few years has revealed, not the existence of widespread spying, not the existence of widespread traitorous activity, but the existence of dissent, the existence of people who refuse to accept the views of the majority without thought and question. Now dissent must be as old as the human species itself. When we look through the pages of history we see evidence of constant change. Our modern civilization has been built by a continuing adaptation to changing circumstances and to new knowledge. Every change is an outcome of new ideas that to begin with are not held by the majority. Change comes from a minority who are able to appreciate the importance of new factors entering into the social organization and who are willing to fight for their views. Change comes from the dissenters, in short. This is why I scout altogether the opinion that the existence of dissent in the United States is a threat to the future of the American people. A community without dissent is well on the way to becoming an ant heap. Indeed one of my strongest aversions to Communism is that it permits no dissent.

Perhaps I should give a few examples. In the previous chapter I believe that my general attitude toward the economic issues between Communism and Capitalism was quite plainly stated. Yet I regard it as my duty to listen to the arguments of a person dissenting from these views, and to argue without becoming doctrinaire or angry. Someone might suggest, for instance, that the timber industry would be in a more favorable situation today if some form of communal control had been exercised in the past—to the effect that timber should not be cut at a faster rate than the rate of natural growth. I would be willing to agree that those people who are employed by the State—by the Post Office shall we say—have not been debased by their services to the community; that they are not to be regarded as a race apart from those of their fellow citizens who are employed by private industry; that they are not a set of submen and subwomen. I would even agree with a communist that the Armed Services should be controlled by the community (i.e., the State), not by private industry.

It will be recalled that the main aim of the chapter is to discuss the all-pervasive influence of communism. What has just been said shows that the identification of this influence is not quite so easy as might at first sight be thought. And this I think agrees with one's general feeling. The widespread dread of Communism is not a precisely formulated argument; it is a largely unformed, unanalyzed impression that in some subtle sinister way our society is being threatened, right through to its innermost fabric. Each one of us I think is coming to feel that all individuality is being hammered out of our lives. More and more as each year passes, we are being required to live as automatons, not as humans. Individual freedom is being lost and it is being lost rapidly. Even a decade or two ago individual expression was much more widespread than it is today, while conditions at the beginning of the present century seem, in this respect, an unattainable ideal.

That this ill-defined feeling arises from something that possesses reality is I am sure correct. But whether it arises from Communism and from the communists appears doubtful to me. I suspect that the whole matter lies on a different level. It lies in a very deep-rooted conflict between the interests of the individual and the interests of the community of which he is a member. To brush off as communist infiltration something that is developing inexorably within modern civilization at this deep level is in my view a most serious mistake, since we are scarcely likely to find the solution to what I am convinced is a crucial social problem if we insist on looking in the wrong place.

It is easy to see how the confusion with Communism has arisen. The suppression of individuality is a matter of deliberate policy in communist countries. Out of this we have come to associate lack of individual freedom with Communism. When we find in our own communities that free individual expression is passing away, we then somewhat naturally tend to think that our troubles are being caused by the designs of the communists. I would be happy if this were indeed the case, since the situation might then be fairly easy to put to rights. But I fear that the basic problem has nothing at all to do with Communism. It is true that the communists are worse afflicted than we are but the problem would still be with us, I think, even if communist beliefs had never been heard of. The problem already lies within ourselves.

It seems to me that whether Man sinks back to barbarism and possibly to extinction, or whether he rises to heights far beyond what we have at present achieved, depends in a large measure on whether we succeed—we of this generation—in understanding and solving the problems that are inherent in the relation of individual and community. Never before have both the dangers and the potential rewards been so great. There can never have been a time when so much depended on the actions of a single generation. For those who like excitement and decision, today is the time to be alive.

The next step to be taken is clear from what has just been said. It is necessary to amplify the whole matter of the relation of man to the society in which he lives. Unfortunately the very statement of the problem, let alone its solution, turns out to be a project of considerable difficulty. An attempt on it must nevertheless be made.

At this stage we shall drop the Communist issue. All that I feel I can usefully say on this has already been said. I must confess that I regard the above discussion as being largely introductory to what is to follow. Now that we have struck a problem that seems capable of leading us to a more significant level of discussion it is important that we should fasten on to it and follow it through to the end.

A bowler at cricket can take as much preparation as he pleases within quite wide limits. In distinction to a baseball pitcher, he is allowed as much of a "run to the wicket" as he likes. In what follows I have allowed myself a long, leisurely run to the wicket. Without simile, I intend to approach the consideration of our present-day world, and of the relation of the individual to the community, through a historical survey. If I were pressed to explain this predilection, I would argue that it is not possible to understand the state of affairs in our own day without some understanding of what has gone before; that society changes with time, and that it is almost useless to try to comprehend its present form unless something of the whole of human evolution is first brought into perspective. Even so, the reader who wishes to fire ahead with the main arguments may care to proceed straightaway to the beginning of Chapter V, or even perhaps to the beginning of Chapter VI.

IV.

The Historical Record

THE FIRST lesson a novice learns in skiing is how to fall properly, for without considerable application and practice we instinctively fall in the wrong way. A few weeks ago I tripped over an obstacle in the dark, an obstacle that normally should not have been there, and which I was not expecting to be there. As I fell I threw out my arms—result: a sprained wrist. Many are the fingers, wrists, and arms that have been broken in this fashion.

While I nursed my wrist I mused on the accident, seeking thereby to wring some degree of profit out of it. Why should evolution have led us into such a thoroughly ungainly action? One would have thought that evolution would by now have taught us the sensible way to fall, by rolling over on one shoulder. Few if any of the other physical reactions of the human body seem at first sight to be so obviously stupid as this matter of falling, falling onto the ground, that is to say. But the situation is quite different if you should happen to fall through a tree. If you fall off a branch, the sensible thing is to fling out your arms with the object of grabbing another branch, just as you instinctively do.

This little diversion provides one of the simplest and most convincing pieces of evidence of the monkey ancestry of Man. It also shows how little Man has changed his monkey make-up.

Perhaps some ten million years ago a chattering monkey-like creature moved around on the Earth, sometimes using legs and sometimes arms. This ambivalence between arms and legs did not persist, however. There was a tendency toward specialization, some creatures coming to use the legs more and more at the expense of the arms, with others coming to adopt the contrary behavior. Those that developed strong legs were naturally led into an upright posture. Not only this but the weakening of the arms made life in the trees less attractive, so these creatures were led to seek a livelihood in the great grassland areas of the world. In contrast, the trees of the forest became increasingly attractive to those who excelled in the development of the arms: these were the creatures who ultimately developed into the arm-swinging apes of the present day.

Conditions must have been extremely difficult for the monkeymen who first moved into the grasslands. They must have found themselves in severe competition with other animals apparently more specialized and better adapted to life in the plains and the hills. Inferior in speed, and unable to match the others in tooth and claw, the monkeymen depended for their survival on the discovery of novel methods of eking out an existence, methods that depended on groups of individuals working together, and on thinking. Even so, existence must have been marginal. The survival of these primitive men was apparently a touch-and-go affair extending probably over several million years.

The study of prehistory extends backward from the present era some half a million years. By the time primitive man emerged on the stage of prehistory he already showed many of the physical characteristics of modern man. Yet his existence was still of the poorest: the total world population was probably no more than half a million, no more than the number of people now resident in Cincinnati, Ohio. The tremendous efflorescence of mankind during the last half million years is emphasized by the contrast with the present world population, which totals around two and a half billion. In contrast to the wonderful tools of the modern world, the tools available to the men of half a million years ago were no more than suitably shaped stones that they managed to find in a natural state, lying to hand on the ground. Gradually over the millennia the idea of actually making tools arose. Instead of relying on finding stones by chance it became possible to fashion them by hand. An interesting point is that two quite different traditions arose, one in which bits were struck off a stone until the required shape was reached and the other in which the bits flaked off a stone themselves served as the tools. The interesting feature of this difference is that the two traditions were geographically separated—the core tools belonged to Africa and Western Europe, and the flake tools to Central Europe and Eurasia. It seems as if we have evidence of two exclusive culture patterns. I like to think that mankind a quarter of a million years ago was rent by a schism that seemed just as important and which lasted far longer than that which separates the Communists and Anti-Communists. I imagine that passions ran very high about which was the "right" way to cut up stones.

For several hundred thousand years Man's progress was extremely slow. Not until about thirty thousand years ago did the first of the great surges take place, the surges that have carried Man to his present remarkable height. Europe was then invaded by men who were much better equipped than those of earlier times. These men had discovered how to make adequate clothing and were thereby able to stay on through the last major advance of the northern ice sheets. They lived in caves, and for food they hunted the mammoth, bison, and woolly rhinoceros, which were driven south by the ice sheet and hence were to be found in considerable numbers near its edge.

An increasing population is indicated by the development of a social organization, an organization that included magic practices and the ritual burial of the dead. Corpses were provided with meat and implements, presumably to assist them to some new existence. Here then we have evidence of the belief in survival after death. Corpses were also placed in special attitudes, a practice that has been followed in subsequent mortuary activities, such as those of the ancient Egyptians and those of the modern American mortician. Already, thirty thousand years ago, man was possessed of superstitious beliefs not substantially different from those that have come down to us today.

The period from 30,000 B.C. to about 10,000 B.C. was particularly rich in the production of new tools, of new ways of life, of art, and of ideas. For the first time, the potentialities of the human brain began to produce outstanding results.

A catalogue of the achievements of the early part of this period must include major improvements in tool-making—tools that could be resharpened when blunted—and the use of bone, ivory, and wood as well as stone. There were now furs for clothing, tents made of hides, and mud huts. These men must have been clever hunters, judging by the great piles of animal bones that still remain to testify to their skill.

Standards of achievement rose steadily until the great Magdalenian culture was attained, the highest achievement of Man in his food-gathering epoch. Tools were now employed for the purpose of making tools, surely a great intellectual achievement. The edges of tools were sharpened by polishing and delicate flaking techniques were developed. The bow and arrow, the spear, and the harpoon and hook for fishing were all invented. Bones were no longer discarded but were burned as fuel. At the zenith of these attainments a population level of perhaps one person per square mile was reached, which approximately equals the population density of the North American Indian before the advent of white men.

Equally interesting is the evidence that relates to the social organization of the Magdalenians. The hunting of large animals required co-operation on a scale something bigger than the family. Trade was carried out over considerable distances, particularly trade in special flints. Magic practices were an important element in Magdalenian life. Corpses were sprinkled with ocher to give them a semblance of life, a practice that survived into the civilized era. There were mystic rites apparently aimed at increasing both human fertility and the fertility of the hunted animals. The special interest attached to these rites arises from the circumstance that they were practiced deep underground inside caves, where they were supplemented by remarkable paintings on the cave walls and by sculptures in clay. In recent years examples of these paintings and sculptures have been discovered in southern France and Spain. By any standards the craftsmanship is high, so high that it is clear that the Magdalenian cave artists were not just casual amateurs. They were apparently a special class of priest-artist. This is a point of no small importance; for it would seem to be the first case in human history of nonproductive individuals being supported out of the food surplus of the general community. These cave artists were perhaps the first example of professionalism.

In spite of great progress in the development of his resources, Magdalenian man was still dependent on food-gathering. He was therefore powerless against changes of environment that reduced the number of animals on which he was dependent for food. When the ice sheet retreated to the north, zones of tundra, forest, and marshland were formed, thereby causing a large shift in the balance of the animal population. This effectively destroyed the basis of the Magdalenian culture; and magic was not able to prevent it. The Magdalenian culture died and with it a large proportion of the population. Only a remnant managed to survive by taking up residence in the new forests and glades, where they eked out a precarious living.

The resources available to mankind are determined by the combination of two factors: knowledge and the potentiality of the environment. The Magdalenians failed to survive because the development of their knowledge did not keep pace with the change of the environment. In this sense their situation was similar to that of the modern world. The rapid exhaustion of high-grade metallic ores and of coal and oil that is going on at the present time will cause a serious change in the future environment of modern man. Unless knowledge advances sufficiently to keep step with this change our descendants are likely to suffer the same fate as the Magdalenians, and that in only a few more centuries.

After this aside let us go back to 10,000 B.C. and follow the remnants of the Magdalenians as they sought a livelihood in the forest glades, and by the sea. Fishing and the capture of wildfowl and small game provided the main food supply. The economy became associated with timber, and as time passed the beginnings of carpentry were made. The dog was domesticated.

But the old population was not left in peace to enjoy even this poor economy. A large-scale movement into Europe of a long-headed, short-statured people succeeded in pushing the descendants of the Magdalenians toward the marginal fringes, where they probably formed the original population referred to in various legends; for example, this was possibly the oldest of the prehistoric populations referred to in Celtic mythology.

It is an interesting speculation as to what ultimately would have happened to the human species if it had been forced to evolve from the culture described above. The likelihood is that things today in Europe would be little different from the old crude timber economy, with its dependence for food on fish and fowl. This economy persisted in some parts of Europe from about 10,000 B.C. to about 3000 B.C. without any great changes taking place, and there seems every reason to suppose that left to itself the same culture would have persisted for at least another five thousand years. The timber culture was not destined, however, to run its course. It was to be absorbed by a new culture from the East; a culture that was based on perhaps the most far-reaching discovery yet made by the human species, the discovery of agriculture. The casual gathering of grasses and plants must, of course, have been carried out in much earlier times; the emphasis here is on the deliberate practice of agriculture. The new economy had reached Asia Minor, Iran, Syria, Turkestan, and the Nile Valley by about 5000 B.C. As a fringe to this development an agricultural economy was also gradually spread through Europe, not reaching some remote parts until about 2500 B.C.

Although the new economy is known to have been practiced some six or seven thousand years ago in the river valleys of the Near East, the actual discoveries of agriculture must have been made at a still earlier date, for in the first archaeological records the system is already well developed. The economy was already of a mixed variety. That is to say, sundry animals were no longer slaughtered on sight but were domesticated. The provision of clothing had been revolutionized: flax and cotton were grown, and wool was obtained from sheep. Primitive looms were invented, querns were used for grinding corn, clay was molded and baked to make pots. Bread was made and, since yeast was used in the bread-making, alcoholic beverages were presumably known.

The village with about a score of separate households formed the unit out of which larger social organizations were constructed. Magic rites once again had a strong hold on the people. But instead of magic being associated with a hunting economy we now find it woven into agriculturalism. Instead of fertility being associated with the birth of hunted animals, the new farmers were concerned with the preservation of the fertility of the soil. The natural cycle of birth in spring, growth in summer and autumn, death in winter, followed by rebirth in spring, was given a religious form. The yearly cycle was thought to arise from the influence of a god, or probably more accurately of a goddess; the onset of winter was explained, not as an outcome of the tilt of the Earth's axis of rotation, but as the death of the goddess.

Since the existence of the goddess could not be established observationally, the next step in the distorted reasoning of these people was to choose a human to represent the goddess; the idea being that the representative should undergo, as far as possible in actuality, the same cycle that the goddess was supposed to undergo. So we have the origin of the pagan spring and autumn festivals, festivals that have indeed come down in disguised forms to modern times; and so we have the reason that underlay the sacrifice of human victims: the death of the goddess required the death of a representative. Quaint as these beliefs might seem, they established such an ascendancy over the outlook of the people that they persisted with only minor modifications for more than five thousand years.

Turning now to more rational matters, the enormous increase of human resources conveyed by the agricultural revolution enabled man for the first time to gain an important measure of control over his environment. But in Europe the consequent advantages were largely canceled out because the new agriculturalists failed to understand the need either for soil fertilization or for crop rotation. A community would settle in a particular district for a limited number of years. When the agricultural methods they employed produced a temporary exhaustion of the soil, the community simply moved on to new land. Instead of developing a rooted agriculturalism the early European farmers were really a sort of agricultural nomad, rather like the American farmers of the last century. The immediate effect was a rapid spread of the new economy. Eventually, however, no more land was left to spread into, and then the trouble started. Men began to fight among themselves for land. Archaeological evidence shows that whereas in the early stages of the new economy there was no preoccupation with weapons of war, ultimately the manufacture of weapons became of prime importance.

Accordingly we picture Europe during most of the three millennia before Christ as a turbulent mass of warring, agriculturally nomadic tribes. Each tribe carried with it its own special complement of gods and goddesses. When one tribe overwhelmed another, the victory was represented as the triumph of one set of divine beings over the other. The gods of the defeated tribe were not entirely forgotten, however; they were taken over into a subservient role in the mythology of the victorious tribe. Thus the beliefs of a tribe tended to become overlaid with layer after layer of divinities, the whole structure being determined by the actual defeats and absorptions of other tribes. This is a circumstance well shown by ancient Celtic legend.

In this seething unrest we see something of the spirit of modern times. It is true that our modern tribes are more populous than those of five thousand years ago, and that today we fight with airplanes and bombs instead of with stone axes, but the tendency for mankind to split itself into rival warring packs is the same. The tendency to fight, murder, and massacre over issues that cannot matter very much in the long run is the same.

The road from the stone ax to the hydrogen bomb is a long one. The first step, the step without which civilization would probably never have got under way, was an outcome of geography. It lay in the astonishing fertility of the lower valleys of several great rivers—the Euphrates, Tigris, Nile, Indus, and Yellow rivers.

The gradual improvement of technique made it eventually possible to drain the lower valleys of these rivers, thereby yielding land of unprecedented richness. Moreover, the problem of land exhaustion that caused so much trouble to the European agriculturalists did not arise, because the periodic flooding of the rivers effectively fertilized the land through the addition of salts dissolved in the river water. Thus these valleys were capable of supporting a genuinely sedentary population of high density. It was on this circumstance that civilization was based.

In terms to be discussed in the next chapter these localized river valleys yielded high "food profits," the profits being disposed of in the support of a nonagrarian population—the

D

essential feature of civilization. Let us now give some consideration to the nonagrarian population, using the Mesopotamian river peoples as our example. The nonagrarian population was made up in two ways. First it was possible to support craftsmen not directly occupied on the land. From these craftsmen came a spate of new discoveries that in themselves tended to increase productivity still further. The invention of wheeled vehicles and of the ox yoke enabled nonhuman muscle power to be employed. Bricks were produced for building, the potter's wheel was invented, and copper was worked. The provision of metal, even of scarce metal, was an important step, since it made possible the production of more durable tools, tools that could easily be given an edge and which could be resharpened.

Surplus production was disposed of in a second way through the setting up of divine establishments. We have seen how the natural yearly crop cycle became associated in the minds of the primitive agriculturalists with the properties of a goddess, and how the yearly birth and death of the goddess became translated into human representation. This translation led to the origin of a class of devotees whose job it was to serve the all-powerful goddess. Now it was customary that the first fruits of the harvest should be brought to the representatives of the goddess in the autumn: this practice is still observed in the Harvest Festivals of the Christian Church. What was then more natural than that a larger and larger proportion of the food surplus of the prosperous river valley people should be brought as a thank-offering to the goddess; and what more natural than that the company of devotees should grow, so that ultimately a considerable divine establishment was formed?

As time went on, the divine establishments were no longer satisfied with gifts, but came to own land of their own, and they came to employ their own workers and craftsmen. Since copper was expensive, they were better able to afford copper tools than the small farmer. Thus the farming methods employed by the large establishments became more efficient than others, and hence the corporations became wealthier still. What was happening has its parallel in the modern business world where the large firm tends to swallow the small one. Down the centuries the divine establishments came to control a larger and ever larger fraction of the wealth of the community. Partly through this economic control, which enabled them to employ a considerable proportion of the craftsmen, and partly through their religious hold over the people, the divine corporations became at last the effective rulers of these river valley communities. A movement that had started as a thanksgiving for the bounty of the Earth had ended by controlling the whole society. This control had two outstanding effects.

In the first place it prevented the advantage of the sharp rise of productivity being entirely swallowed up by a corresponding rise of population. The divine establishments, with only a small fraction of the total population to support, took to themselves a substantial fraction of the total productivity. Thus even if the rest of the production was parceled out among the maximum number of people that could be kept alive with it, the total population of the community had perforce to remain appreciably less than the number that might otherwise have arisen if the divine production had also been shared around equally. In bad times the corporations could therefore prevent a collapse of society, since they could disburse sufficient bounty to keep the people alive: the great goddess could come to the rescue of her starving people. In this way the community was able to ride out a temporary series of exceptionally poor harvests. By taking enormously more than their "fair share" of the total production the devotees of the goddess were able to stabilize the economy. Equal shares all around would probably have produced a collapse in a few centuries, whereas the activities of the divine establishments enabled the whole system to last, from its early beginnings in about 5000 B.C. down to about 3000 B.C.

This temple economy also supplied an important service to human knowledge. Large inventories were compiled to describe the property of the goddess. Since these inventories had to be understandable, not to one individual only, but to the divine clerks in general, writing was invented. Moreover, since numbers were also required by the divine inventories, and since calculations had to be performed, the beginnings of arithmetic were made. In short, the mystic corporations supplied for intellectual activity what the craftsmen were supplying in the practical field. Nor were these intellectual activities negligible; the arithmetical achievements reached the level of multiplication, an invention that was scarcely to be paralleled in any of the later civilizations of the ancient world. The number 60, which was used as a base by these early calculators, has infiltrated through into modern times in many ways; in the number of minutes to the hour, for instance.

It is of interest at this stage to inquire into a deeper issue. Why did the people of this first civilization not succeed in making the further discoveries on which our modern civilization rests? They had, be it noted, done so much; they and their forerunners had invented almost the whole of agriculture, in which they had invented the basis of mechanical development; they had invented the beginning of metallurgy; and in the intellectual field they could write and calculate. Compared with what had already been achieved, the further knowledge that would have enabled civilization to gain an enormous additional momentum was not unduly great; but it was not forthcoming. Instead, the first civilization was to drift on and on until it broke up about 3000 B.C., presumably as a result of unduly adverse circumstances. From 5000 B.C. onward there was a steady change of climate. As a consequence, conditions in the Mesopotamian River valleys may well have become steadily less advantageous. The stability induced by the temple economy was apparently sufficient, however, to resist the gradual deterioration, but evidently was not sufficient to resist some final disruptive influence. This may have happened in a number of ways: there may have been a long sequence of unprecedentedly bad harvests; there may have been plagues of insects that attacked the crops; some physical disease may have struck down the people; there are many ways in which a society that seeks only to preserve the *status quo* can be destroyed by an unusual circumstance. The interesting point is not so much the precise events that caused the collapse of the first civilization—this was inevitable once fossilization had set in; the question is: why should the addition to knowledge have stopped after such a fair beginning?

The answer would seem to lie partly in the inability of the people to rid themselves of primitive magical beliefs. When the study of astronomy showed that the alternation of the seasons of the year can adequately be explained in terms of the tilt of the Earth's axis, the rational step would have been to discard the old hocus-pocus about the activities of a goddess. This was not done, probably because the very people who were in a position to denounce the old views were themselves profiting enormously from the naïveté of the popular outlook. Instead, the divine clerks seem to have become even more addicted to magic practices; for example, astrology became preferred to astronomy.

Perhaps we should not overemphasize this tendency toward magic practices; for in their early developments both science and mathematics had themselves something of a magical air: it is likely that only people with inclinations toward magic would indeed have conceived of these early developments. Not until recent times did men learn how to distinguish between the general potentialities of science and the charlatanic claims of the magician. Even to Newton the distinction was not clear. It has been fashionable to express surprise that the man who produced the great *Principia* should also have dabbled in alchemy and in the numerological interpretation of ancient writings. If Newton had not had magical leanings, however, if he had not held a strong belief in the possibility of gaining a greater measure of predictability of the future, it is likely that he would never have had the imagination to conceive the enormous scope of the *Principia*.

Let us now come to the second reason why the ancient Mesopotamian civilization failed to continue the accumulation of knowledge. The vital junction between the work of the craftsman and the achievements of the intellectual was never made, and for a reason that is readily understandable. In the divine corporations craftsmen were allotted a lowly position. Outside the corporations craftsmen, it is true, had a fair measure of independence; but as the corporations gained increasing power the individual craftsman was gradually forced out of business, so to speak; and proportionately to his decline there was a decline in invention. The great period of invention belonged to the days of independence: dependence brought stultification. The divine clerks, on whom intellectual progress depended, had much too high an opinion of themselves to form a partnership on equal terms with the humble craftsmen. So the two stayed apart, and without their combination both became sterile: craftsmen were to descend, first into humble service, and then into outright slavery; intellectual activities were to degenerate into the fruitless pursuit of magical beliefs. So partly from a failure of social organization, and partly because the brains of the people became caught up in the wrong concepts, this early civilization, which began with such rich promise, was to come to nought; or more exactly its discoveries were not to bear fruit until they had passed from one equally evanescent civilization to another over a period of more than four millennia. It was not until the second millennium after Christ that mankind was again to be favored with conditions as propitious as this first civilization enjoyed. Fortunately when the next great opportunity came the same mistake was not repeated.

It is interesting to follow the Mesopotamian civilization just a little further. We have already seen how this civilization became fossilized, and how ultimately it became disrupted by some untoward occurrence. Now once a civilization begins to disintegrate, disintegration feeds on itself. Men fight amongst themselves instead of engaging in productive activities; farmers can no longer work peaceably in the fields; and plunder seems the surest way to survival. The activities of civilized Man are so related to the social organization, the whole machinery of which is so complicated, that disruption beyond a certain point leads to utter chaos; chaos on a vastly greater scale than could ever have occurred to Man in his older nomadic existence, or in the early days of the agricultural economy, or even in the tribal state. This instability is a rooted property of civilization.

Let us continue these abstract considerations by inquiring into the outcome of a wholesale disruption of civilization. We ask: what ultimate losses are caused by such a disintegration? Certainly the natural advantages of the environment are not lost: the valleys of the Euphrates and Tigris were just as fertile after the first breakdown of Mesopotamian civilization as they were before. So a decline of resources could occur only if knowledge was lost. Here we reach perhaps the most important determining factor in Man's evolution: knowledge is more durable than a social organization. A social organization may be utterly smashed, but the tendency is for the knowledge that has been won to survive. The reason for this is clear: it is very hard to originate a really new idea; in contrast, it is comparatively easy to copy something new; even a slight hint is a great help to making a new step. Now when a civilization collapses, enough knowledge usually survives to make it easy for subsequent generations to rediscover anything that at first sight may seem to have been lost. It was in such a way that in the fourteenth and fifteenth centuries A.D. our modern civilization was able to acquire the learning of the ancient world so readily.

The above remarks lead us to a crucial proposition: so long as a civilization does not collapse through a worsening of the environment, collapse does not lead to any important ultimate reduction of resources. In other words, the disintegration of a civilization leads to a reduction of population and to the destruction of a social organization, and that is all.

We return now to the valleys of the Tigris and Euphrates. The collapse of the first civilization produced a reduction of population and it smashed the old temple economy, but it did not produce any lasting destruction of resources. It follows that the opportunity was presented for a re-expansion back to the former level of population.

The reformation did not result, however, in a social system with any advantage over the previous organization. Imagine first the emergence of a number of individuals who managed to come out of the chaos better off than their fellows: chaos produces random effects that are certain to throw up a number of particularly favored people. Then we imagine a process of elimination in the competition for power among these favored individuals; this process leading in the course of time to a small group that gained effective control of the whole society. In the last stage the struggle continued among this small group, until finally one person or one family emerged victorious and controlled the whole of the community. To impress his power still further, the leader took upon himself the attributes of the chief divinity of the old civilization, thereby turning any superstitions that had survived the catastrophe to his personal advantage. In this way we reach a social organization dominated by a pushing, warlike individual, and backed by the old religious prejudices.

It is of course true that this organization is not the only one that might have arisen out of the chaos. A partial democracy might have grown up with a comparatively large number of prosperous families of equal status living in peace with each other. Such an evolution, even on the face of it, is much less probable than the sort of development described in the previous paragraph. Indeed, so far as I am aware, no democracy of this sort has ever arisen after a period of really serious decline leading to social chaos. Democracies have occurred in the world, but they have never arisen from a state of entire social disruption. Should our modern civilization collapse, it is I think unlikely that democracy will rise again from the ruins.

Now what happens ultimately to the process of re-expansion? Just as the old divine corporations took an undue share of the total productivity and thereby introduced a tendency toward social stability, so did the new human warrior-god apportion an undue share of the productivity to himself. It would seem, however, that the unfair share of the warrior-god was less than that which had been gobbled up by the temple economy. Hence the new regime possessed a smaller stability factor than the old one. So what was to prevent the new civilization breaking up as the first civilization had broken up? What was to prevent the population rising so close to the maximum supportable number that some untoward happening would induce the onset of a second disintegration? Evidently there was nothing to prevent such a second disintegration, since population control was not practiced. Without population control, the onset of the disruptive phase of civilization cannot be prevented merely by the extension of resources, although of course the moment of disintegration can be postponed thereby.

Thus we anticipate a second collapse of civilization. This indeed occurred. What then, we may ask, was to prevent the whole cycle being repeated once again? What was to stop a new scramble for leadership, a rising population ultimately overloading the economy, a search abroad for new resources; warfare plus economic instability leading to a further collapse; a new period of reorganization and expansion? What indeed was to prevent this cycle from being repeated endlessly? Apparently there was very little to prevent it, since in point of fact the history of the three thousand years before Christ in Mesopotamia and the Near East is simply a history of the repetitions of this cycle. And in this, at last, we reach the most characteristic feature of civilization, the tendency to fall into a cyclic progression of integration and disintegration.

What we are now saying is really very simple, namely that a civilized society tends to overpopulate its nonagrarian component. When food supplies become short the correct inference is not drawn—that the nonproductive section of the community should be slowly reduced. Instead the temptation is to raise an army in order to seize someone else's food. This only makes matters worse, because the raising of an army only increases the nonproductive component still further. In this event wars, famines, and collapse become inevitable.

To continue with our historical discussion, it was the Earth itself that saved the situation, the wide spaces of the Earth. In their search for increased food supplies the early civilizations sent their armies into ever wider territories. They carried with them the agricultural techniques and knowledge of the river valley peoples. In this way civilization spread gradually to the West, to the Mediterranean. So was the way prepared for a general change of climate that took place gradually during the three millennia before Christ. An increasing desiccation of the territory of the Near East combined with incessant warring of the old civilizations led eventually to a removal of the center of civilization to the Mediterranean. The torch was taken up first by the Greeks and then by the Romans.

But both the Roman and the Greek civilizations were subject to the contradictions that have beset all agrarian economies, excepting only the limited territories of the river valleys where civilization was born. Low "food profits" inadequate to provide for a swelling nonproductive population, armies draining away the small food surpluses, war—these were the causes of the decline of Greece. Glorious Greece was replete with wise words, but it ill understood the cause of its own disease. The Romans managed better than the Greeks. They were fortunate in coming to control pretty much the whole of the then known world. Everyone paid tribute to Rome. This and a succession of able administrators enabled Roman civilization to persist for a remarkably long time. Rome perhaps represented the ultimate height that humanity would ever have reached if inanimate energy from coal and oil had not become increasingly available. Without inanimate energy not even Rome could survive however.

When the collapse came, around A.D. 400, it almost seemed as if civilization had perished for good and all. The Roman Empire had been so widespread that the collapse apparently affected all conceivable places where civilization might flourish. Yet within another fifteen hundred years civilization was to re-emerge even more decisively and notably than ever before. Mankind was to make its greatest surge forward since the invention of agriculture. When was the foundation of modern civilization laid? Curiously enough in the age about which we know least, from about A.D. 900 to A.D. 1200. This was the feudal age in Europe, in its roots a survival from Roman times. Feudalism has often been described as a productively inefficient system, but in this lay one of its outstandingly important features, for inefficiency in food production meant that the feudal population was not nearly so large as it could, and would, have been if more efficient methods had been used. So that when the feudal system ultimately broke down and better agricultural techniques were introduced the opportunity for a considerable expansion of population arose. It was on this expansion that our modern civilization was founded.

This was not all however. Feudalism did not collapse until just the right moment. It did not collapse until a whole series of technological inventions had been made, inventions that were to prepare the way for the effective use of inanimate energy. I think it is likely that none of the Old World civilizations, neither the Greeks nor the Romans, were able to make the transition from human and animal muscle power to machine power because the collapse of one civilization was followed too quickly by the re-emergence of another. This never allowed craftsmen the stability and peace of mind that was necessary for developing the minor technological inventions that the older civilizations lacked. In contrast the feudal period provided several centuries of valuable concentration on mechanical problems.

Owing to the low feudal population, human labor was never common and was indeed sometimes scarce. The effect of a plague, for example, would produce a temporary lowering of population and hence would stimulate a demand for human labor. Besides tending to emphasize the importance of the individual, such scarcities prompted a search for mechanical methods of replacing human muscle power. Thus the medieval world was machine-conscious in a way that the slave civilizations of the ancient world had never been. The windmill, the mechanical saw, the forge with tilt hammer were invented in the twelfth century, along with the wheelbarrow, window glass, the domestic chimney, candles, and paved roads. Spectacles, the wheeled plow with moldboard, and the ship's rudder came in the thirteenth century; lock gates on the Dutch canals and other advances of practical hydraulics, gunpowder, and the grandfather clock came in the fourteenth century. Printing was the outstanding contribution of the fifteenth century.

Alongside these practical developments, progress was also being made in abstract thought. During the Dark Ages the ancient knowledge had in a large measure been preserved by the Church; and what had been lost was quickly refound or rediscovered. More particularly, the problem of the dynamics of moving bodies began to attract serious attention in the fourteenth century. The decision of the new science to choose dynamics as its starting point was propitious. The precise data obtained from the flight of cannonballs when added to astronomical knowledge provided a body of information superior to that available to the ancient world. It was on these data that the new investigations were based. The work culminated in the discoveries of Newton, which not only solved the general problem of dynamics, thereby taking Man's intellectual achievement one clear step beyond that of the Greeks, but supplied the pattern for all subsequent scientific developments. From then onward, instead of stumbling in a maze, science had a path to follow.

In spite of the great Newtonian triumph the junction between practice and intellect, the junction that was so sadly lacking in the ancient world, did not come mainly from the intellectual side. The intellectual was still disinclined to reach downward—as he saw it—to the craftsman. Once again the opportunity might have slipped by, had it not been for the changed outlook of the craftsman. The craftsman was now no longer a slave to be ordered around at his master's pleasure. The craftsman emerged from the Middle Ages with a new-found respect in himself. He was ambitious, and he had confidence—are we not all equal in the sight of God? He formed guilds to promote skill in his craft and to preserve himself from exploitation. Above all he was able to reach out to the intellectual discoveries of the new science, which were now readily available to him through the invention of printing. At first in a vague form, and then with increasingly more precision, the craftsman began to pick up the elements of the new science. The outcome of the long-delayed union of theory and practice came in the eighteenth century with the spate of mechanical discoveries that made way for the industrial development that has since become the outstanding characteristic of modern civilization. This social explosion, it may be noted, required more than three centuries of development from its beginning, and four centuries before it began to yield really important results. That society did not run into the disintegrative phase of the civilization cycle long before the end of four centuries we owe to the great amount of slack that was created in feudal times: it was due to the population then falling so low that four centuries of expansion were permitted to us. Industrialism has further added enormously to human resources, both directly and by enabling the resources of the Americas to be developed. The recent rise of populations, to be noted in a later chapter, was made possible by this further addition to human resources.

V.

The Significance of Industrialism

IT MIGHT seem as if the spread of industrialism has reduced the human individual to a cipher, so that one might suspect that the elucidation of our social problem lies in the nature of industrialism. In a sense this is correct, but only in a limited sense. Certainly a strong argument can be put forward to show that industrialism is the immediate agency whereby individual personality has been submerged. It would be interesting to trace how artistic forms have been changed by the incidence of industrialism from serenity to desperation and defiance. Although this is a subject that would repay a close historical study, such a survey would be out of place here. It is sufficient to notice that a drastic change in artistic forms is a sure indication that a crucial change of social organization has taken place. It may be remarked that the collapse of English music in the eighteenth century had nothing at all to do with Communism. Yet in this collapse we have preliminary symptoms of the disease of our own times. We begin to see that deeper currents are flowing than those of Communism.

Now to consider industrialism in its simplest aspects. The

E

essence of industrialism lies in replacing human muscle power by the motive power of machines. Steam power, the earliest development, had the characteristic that the most efficient way of obtaining a substantial power supply was from one large machine, not from many small ones. This meant that it was desirable to work a whole lot of processing machinery from one steam engine. Thus in the textile industry it was desirable to work a large number of looms from one power source, rather than to have a separate steam engine for each loom. The natural corollary of this was the development of the factory system.

Discoveries in electricity largely reversed the situation. Since it is easy to carry electricity over a considerable distance, there is no particular reason why each processing machine should not be powered by its own electric motor. Indeed from many points of view this is the best arrangement: different types of processing machines have different load characteristics, so that in many ways it is better to provide each one with a suitably designed motor than to have them all operated by the same power source. Thus it might have been expected that with the coming of electricity there would be a drift away from the factory system. To some extent this has happened: today many businesses are competently handled in small workshops. Even in large concerns it is often found that work is done not in one great room but in many separate workshops. Nevertheless the factory system has not died out, it is more strongly entrenched today than it ever was.

The reason for this continuation differs from the original reason that fostered the factory system. It lies no longer in the nature of the power source, but in an organizational property of the factory system. It was discovered that when a large number of people work together in some concern it is more efficient for each man to do just one operation than to spread his activities over a wide range—by more efficient I mean that production is thereby increased. The outcome of this discovery was the mass-production system.

Mass production brought many evils in its train. By reducing the work required from a man to some single, readily learned operation, it effectively stamped out craftsmanship. This in turn led to a deep-rooted dissatisfaction in those who worked under the system: it is from many points of view as important that a man should feel there is some one genuinely skillful activity he does uncommonly well, as that he should be given an adequate food supply. In past times it was craftsmanship that mainly provided this necessity. When craftsmanship was destroyed by the mass-production system obvious consequences arose. Men were no longer interested in their work. It became a prime concern to do as little as possible, and to seek the highest possible pay in return for it.

Now what can be done about all this? For many years the mass-production system seemed inevitable to modern industrialization. To dispense with it would enormously reduce efficiency, and in a competitive world this was not to be thought of. Thus it seemed that society had worked itself into a state where prosperity could only be achieved at the expense of a psychological deterioration in the majority of factory workers. All this is now in the process of being changed. To understand the tremendous revolution of industrial technique that is being ushered in today, it may be pointed out that the psychological deterioration associated with mass production arises from the sheer repetitiveness of the work. The human brain is not well designed for the exact repetition of any activity that requires conscious thought. Monotony must inevitably arise and given sufficient monotony general deterioration must follow. The brain is at its best when called on, not to repeat exactly a particular task, but to repeat it with slight but essential variations.

Modern developments in electronics have now reached the stage where it is possible to design an electrical machine that can control any exactly repeated activity, no matter how complicated it may be. It seems possible, for instance, to design an electrical machine that could control all the repeated activity of an automobile assembly works. This means that the dead monotony of mass-production work is a disease that can be cured.

This is the first of two outstandingly hopeful features. To say that industrialism has hopeful features may possibly seem to be in contradiction to the opening remarks of the present chapter. But as one comes more and more to realize, nothing in human affairs can be represented in simple black and white. Industrialism has highly objectionable characteristics but it also has other properties that may eventually be turned to great advantage. Our aim must be to sift out what is good and to leave behind what is bad, although to achieve this completely is probably an unobtainable ideal. But we can do very much better than we are doing at present.

Let us go on to consider the second hopeful possibility. Human life is based on the production of food; and in order to produce food, work has to be done. In an agrarian society the work is supplied by the muscle power of animals, human and otherwise. Now in order to be able to work, animals must consume food. So in an agrarian society food has to be consumed in order to produce food. This raises an important question: what is the profit? How much more food do we get out than we put in?

The organization of human society that we call "civilization" depends on the answer to this question, for the "profit" from the agricultural cycle is the driving force of civilization. The profit is used to provide for the builders of towns, for smiths and other craftsmen who in turn supply the workers on the land with implements. Only when a man is free from the immediate labor of producing food for himself and his family is it possible for him to give sufficient time and thought to the multitude of problems on the solution of which civilization depends.

Now the profits in an agrarian society are determined quite sensitively by the quality of the land that is being farmed. Medieval Europe was farmed at a modest level of profit, perhaps a profit of some 10 or 15 per cent, in contrast with modern profits which sometimes run into many thousands of per cent. The Greek and Roman civilizations were likewise based on a modest return of some 10 or 20 per cent. To arrive at anything comparable with modern conditions we have to go back some six thousand years when the first civilizations were starting up in the extremely fertile valleys of Mesopotamia, in the Nile Valley, and the valleys of the Indus and the Yellow rivers. It was indeed because Man was able to find a few spots on the Earth where enormous profits were to be made that civilization was ever able to get under way. Once started it was possible to continue at a much lower level, but to get started something quite exceptional was necessary: if the Earth had not possessed a few outstandingly exceptional localities it is fairly certain that civilization would not have occurred, and Man would still be everywhere leading the barbaric existence of the nomad. Although the territory of the United States possesses in a large measure all the requisites of modern civilization it does not possess the kind of spot where civilization could have been born.

Now a word of explanation as to why modern food profits are so vastly higher than they were in the agrarian societies of former times. The work that has to be done to produce food is no longer mainly supplied by animals. The work is now done by machines, and the energy consumed by the machines is derived from coal, oil, and hydroelectric power. Today we no longer use food to supply the energy that is consumed in the working of a farm.

We shall refer to energy derived from coal, oil, etc. as inanimate energy thereby distinguishing it from the energy derived from food, which comes from living things.

The availability of vast stores of inanimate energy has greatly reduced the number of people required to farm a particular territory. Since human muscle power is no longer required in any appreciable degree the number of men who are required to produce a given quantity of food is now very much less than it used to be. In former times, in the old agrarian civilization, those who were fortunate enough to be supported out of the meager food surplus used to disparage the farmer on whom so much depended. It was indeed from these earlier times that the idea of the "country yokel" comes, the idea of the farmer as a clumping clod. But there is nothing of the clod about the modern farmer, who has to be every bit as much a thinker and organizer as the producer of manufactured goods. The change from the farmer as a laborer to the farmer as an organizer epitomizes the change from an agrarian to an industrial civilization.

We must now throw a complication into the argument. When we talked of "modern conditions," the conditions I had in mind were those occurring in the industrialized nations of the West. It must next be said that these conditions even today are still the exception rather than the rule. The great majority of humanity still live under the old agrarian system. The vast populations of Asia still operate under a system of very small food profits.

It seems astonishing that so little attention is paid to this crucial difference in the conduct of international politics. The Asiatic peoples are said to be antiwhite, anticolonial in their outlook, and in some cases procommunist. But surely the transition from an agrarian to an industrial organization must be accounted as an issue of much greater significance than these? The question may not be discussed openly and consciously but it must lie at the root of much that has happened in recent years: I suspect the desire for increased food profits to be the cause of the apparently intractable attitude of many Asians.

Now although it can scarcely be doubted that in the years to come there will be a trend toward industrialism in Asia, I think we are inclined to underestimate the difficulties that will be encountered in bringing this about. Industrialization escaped the classical civilizations entirely. This was not due to any lack of intelligence or enterprise, but because the necessary factors did not happen to combine together in a favorable way. It is true that once industrialism had happened in Europe its spread to other parts of the Earth was a much less difficult matter. Early American industrialization was much assisted, for instance, by ideas from Europe. Even so, the onset of industrialism in America would have been difficult and much delayed if capital had not been forthcoming from Europe, notably from England.

Ideas are available to Asia in plenty, but capital is not; and without a large provision of capital, industrialization will be a long and difficult process. The necessity for capital is easy to understand. To effect industrialization on any worth-while scale a large number of people are required to leave the land in order to take up work in towns, mines, and factories. But in an agrarian society a large number of people cannot be made available for this (or cannot be made available without great hardship), for the reason that the food profits are so low —to keep up the production of food at the necessary level in an agrarian society almost everyone must work on the land. It is here that the provision of external capital becomes of vital importance. The capital may be thought of as food received from outside that serves to make good the internal deficiency that must occur during the transition to industrialism. The external supply of capital, or more fundamentally of food, need only be temporary, since once industrialism gets under way the internal food profits begin to rise very steeply: expressed differently, once machine power replaces human muscle power the number of people required to work on the land greatly decreases, so that the former shortage of agricultural labor disappears.

Where one wonders is Asia to receive the enormous supply of capital that will be necessary if industrialization is to be made a reasonably practicable proposition? In particular where is China, the Asian nation with perhaps the greatest natural resources, to obtain a large supply of capital? From Russia? I doubt it for the reason that Russian industrialization itself is so far only a partial success, as can be seen from the fact that the food profits (the essence of industrialism) are not nearly so high in Russia as they are in America or in Western Europe. I am strongly of the opinion that there is only one source in the world from which an adequate capital provision can possibly be obtained, and that is from the United States.

If this analysis is correct, it follows that present United States policy in regard to China is seriously miscalculated. Wars and threats of wars are not likely to have anything like the psychological force that an appropriately directed economic policy might have. The Chinese have very little to lose by war, whereas America has a great deal to lose. War brings death and misery. To the Chinese people this would be nothing new since all Asia has been experiencing death and misery for centuries. The Chinese must surely come to regard the possibility of an escape from their present abysmal conditions as an issue of outstanding importance. Since the key is held by the United States, it is clear that without any question of a resort to force the West possesses an extremely strong bargaining position. Indeed I do not think that any stronger position is needed, or could or should be hoped for.

The historical record shows that from a strictly profit-and-loss point of view war is a singularly unrepaying activity. Rich harvests it is true have sometimes been reaped by barbaric peoples when on occasion they have managed to attack civilized peoples successfully. But occasions where war has paid good dividends to civilization are very rare. The temptation that war offered to agrarian societies is nevertheless fairly easy to understand.

When food profits are low there is a persistent danger of the nonproductive section of the population growing too numerous. Only a small group can adequately be supported out of the small food surplus of an agrarian community; and throughout history this number has all too readily been exceeded. When this happened the temptation was to grab the food surplus of some other community—by war.

But this policy scarcely ever paid, for the reason that when every community does the same thing, when every community is forced to maintain an army for purposes both of attack and defense, the only real effect is that every community adds to its burden, an addition that is measured by the number of persons who thus become engaged in permanent military duties.

Another point also induced instability into the old agrarian civilizations: in times of food shortage—and throughout history food has mostly been in short supply—the very last people to suffer were the soldiers and their leaders; for the reason that they could always seize what food was available by main force. This led to the farm workers becoming inadequately nourished, and consequently to a decline in the output of food. In this way shortage led progressively to greater shortage. Thus did many of the civilizations of the past decay and collapse.

Industrial civilization resembles agrarian civilization in that war also does not pay. Indeed, while I can understand why the old agrarian civilizations were tempted much to their cost into war, I cannot see any reason at all why an industrial community should be so tempted. Nothing is plainer than that war is now entirely pointless. An industrial community enjoys large food profits. There is accordingly little reason why such a community should worry itself about snatching someone else's profits, particularly the meager profits of an agrarian community. And nothing is surer than that war between two industrial societies will lead to both losing their profits.

This is not a conventional view. Industrial nations are still organizing their affairs in much the same way that the old agrarian civilizations did. I believe this to be a matter of inertia: industrialism is so recent in its impact on the world that not sufficient time has yet elapsed for any really new adjustments to be made; we are still attempting to apply ideas and beliefs descended from old agrarian times. This maladjustment has produced tragic but ludicrous situations. Consider for instance the case of Germany. There can be little doubt that if Germany had been content to pursue a policy of economic consolidation, instead of one of military aggrandizement, in the years between 1910 and 1950, she would today be one of the dominant nations of the world. Granted the strength of Germany in 1910, there was just one way by which Germans could fail in the ambition to make themselves masters of Europe, and that was the way they actually adopted, of declaring war on the world twice.

There seems to me to be just one way by which the United States can fail to remain the dominant nation in the world during the next century, and that is through being disastrously involved in war. The years in which the United States built itself into the leading nation were years of economic development, not years of incessant fighting: the great climb from a backwoods territory to the vanguard of civilization was achieved with scarcely any standing army at all. Yet no sooner does the United States emerge as the main character on the world's stage, than a clamor arises that the sword shall be buckled on, and the same old policy of push-and-tug adopted that has brought down in ruins all the great powers and civilizations of the past.

The discussion of the present chapter has now come full circle. We started by noting some of the deleterious psychological effects of the incidence of industrialism. We now see that these effects may well be due to our own inability to adapt ourselves to the conditions of industrialism: we are approaching the problems of industrialism equipped with minds that are dominated by the worst features of agrarianism. This shows itself most notably in our attitude toward war. Instead of realizing that war is antipathetic to industrialism we continue to view the world situation in the fashion of the ancient civilizations.

Civilization depends on food profits, on those who work on the land being able to produce a surplus of food wherewith to provide for the nonfarming section of the population, from whom must come the multifarious activities on which civilization depends. So long as food profits were low, civilization was never able to work very well—war, famine, decay, and collapse being of frequent incidence. This difficulty has been conquered at any rate in principle by the modern age, the age in which human muscle power has been superseded by machine power. The enormous food profits of the modern era open the way to an entirely new concept of life. But so far we have not been able to take full advantage of these favorable new developments, for the reason that we are attempting to deal with new problems with old minds. Our minds are fossilized in the ancient pattern. This shows itself nowhere more plainly than in our attitude toward war, which in its emotional content scarcely seems to have advanced beyond the days of Sargon.

It does not follow that because the diagnosis is clear the cure must be easy. Modern man seems to be thoroughly out of tune with his environment. Instead of reaping the rich rewards that could conceivably have fallen to our lot, we are apparently determined to fritter our good fortune away. Such a situation is not to be altered by the changing of a few details.

Rather must we bring our whole mental outlook under review. I think that we must try to understand how we came to hold our present ideas. And we must question whether it is we who control these ideas or whether it is the ideas that control us. This is the issue that I wish to consider in the next chapter.

VI.

The Thing

THE HISTORICAL survey of Chapter IV raises an outstanding problem. Why has Mankind effloresced in such an amazing fashion during the last six or seven thousand years? What lies behind the astonishing development from primitive barbarism to modern civilization? Only reasons of the utmost cogency can, I believe, provide an explanation of Man's extraordinary upsurge.

If this be granted, then we can surely argue that the same forces that have produced the upsurge must still persist today; and that any worth-while understanding of our modern life must make a full concession to these forces. It seems well-nigh certain that the self-same dynamic qualities that have driven mankind in the past will continue to drive him in the future. Clearly then if we can discover from our examination of the past just where the driving power came from, we shall have gone far toward understanding how human society is likely to change in the future. Since we are quite evidently being swept along by an extremely powerful current it is important to understand where the current derives its force from, and where it is flowing to.

Let me come instantly to where I believe the real solution to be: in the accumulation of knowledge. The clue to the matter was contained in a remark already made in Chapter IV when we said that knowledge is more durable than a civilization. Knowledge has two qualities that make its importance pre-eminent. It is both durable and cumulative.

The nature of knowledge is not simple. Knowledge does not consist of just a vast library of textbooks. A library is a symbol, a symbol that people exist who can write the books it contains, that people can read the books with understanding, and that people want to read the books. When these essential factors no longer exist, the formal aspect of knowledge as exemplified in the library becomes a meaningless symbol. The great library of Alexandria was a meaningless symbol to the invading Mohammedans. They burnt it.

Knowledge is much better described as an organizational state of society. I think that at first sight we do not realize how deep this organization goes. Even the most gifted individual carries in his head only a fragment of the total of all knowledge. Yet consider how perfectly the contributions of a myriad of individuals are matched together, so perfectly that the structure of knowledge forms one harmonious whole, symbolized indeed in our great libraries. The word "structure" here is not inapt, for rather as atoms build themselves into material substances so knowledge is a structure built out of ourselves as the units.

At this stage it is necessary to introduce the idea that a

structure is something more than the units out of which it is built. A fine building is something more than the pile of bricks out of which it is constructed. If you do not believe this then try the following experiment for yourself. First find out what your house is worth. Then knock it carefully to pieces and see whether you can get as much money for the bits. When we buy a house we pay not only for the materials but also for the structural element. The same is true of every manufactured article. In a similar way knowledge is something more than the individuals whose aggregation together is the essence of knowledge. In my view it is just here that the clue to the control of human affairs lies. It is this structural element, this something more, that drives us along.

The ways of matter are unimaginably wonderful. Until a few years ago it was thought that all matter could be broken down into four basic units—the two heavy particles, the neutron and the proton, the lightweight electron, and the fleeting neutrino. These particles together with three influences which they are believed to radiate—the nuclear influence of the proton and neutron, the electric influence of the proton and electron, and the gravitational influence of all four particles—were thought to control the properties of the Universe. It is coming to be realized that this picture was altogether too simple. Rather does it seem that the neutron and the proton may already be complicated structures built out of an as yet unidentified component. It is also possible that the influences radiated by matter may contain, in addition to the three already mentioned, a fourth influence whereby matter is able to

F

create itself. Each influence plays an important part in enabling matter to build itself into remarkable structures.

Protons and neutrons build themselves into structures. These
structures are the nuclei of the atoms. Atomic nuclei together
with electrons build themselves into atoms. Thus atoms, once
thought to represent the indestructible units of matter, already
represent two and probably three (if not more) structural
steps. Atoms build themselves into molecules. Molecules under
the conditions of temperature occurring on the Earth build
themselves into a great variety of substances. Perhaps the most
remarkable is the living cell, able to reproduce itself in the
presence of suitable chemical foods. Nor does the series of
structural steps stop with the living cell. Living cells are able
to build themselves into structures. These are the plants and
animals. A word about the difference between plants and
animals may be appropriate. Plants are able to build living
cells out of comparatively simple molecules, so simple that
there are usually plenty on hand. Consequently plants do not
have to move around from place to place in search of food.
Animals on the other hand require much more complicated
foods in order to build the cells of which they are composed.
The foods required by animals are indeed so complex that
there is never a sufficiency in a particular location. Only by
moving around, so as to gather food over a wide area, can
animals sustain themselves.

At no stage are we more emotionally aware of the importance of structure than in the step from the single living cell to
the structure built out of cells. The basic cellular component
of a human is no more remarkable in itself than the basic com-

ponent of a turnip. It is in the human structure that the remarkable features lie. But the building process does not end with the human structure, for in the development of knowledge we have a superstructure built out of humans themselves as the units.

Other animals also possess superstructures. The most singular are to be found among the insects, notably ants and bees. Birds too show a considerable organized mass activity. If we except Man, the organization of mammals scarcely approaches that which has been achieved by insects or by birds. But Man has outstripped all others in the complexity of his organization, and in this lies his strength and dominance. Humans taken singly as individuals would scarcely constitute a serious threat to other animals. Humans co-operating together are overwhelming.

Now I imagine that the sociologist and historian will probably wish to quarrel with what I have said. Not with the existence of a formidable human superstructure, but with my identification of the superstructure with knowledge rather than with the social aspects of human behavior. It is undoubted that there are other features of the human superstructure, features of a social nature—rights of property, marriage customs, religions, racial temperaments, culture patterns, and the like. It is customary for these social factors to be thought of outstanding importance, and for knowledge to be regarded as subsidiary. In my view this is a correct expression of our personal wishes and prejudices, of what on an emotional basis we would like to believe. But I do not think that it represents an objective assessment of the situation. Rather does it seem to me that so far as human destiny is concerned the personal factors matter scarcely at all. The control of the trend of major events belongs to knowledge. However much we may dislike this conclusion, I am sure that none other will stand up to rational test (i.e., will yield correct predictions about the future course of events). In my opinion the reason why social studies have so far had little influence on human affairs, as compared with the physical sciences for instance, is that most social studies are simply on the wrong track. In being concerned with the wishes and desires of people they are chasing a will-o'-the-wisp. We shall come nearer a correct assessment of the situation if we concentrate on the textbooks in our library.

This issue is so crucial that it is worth discussing arguments for it at some length. Bluntly, I fail to see any very great difference between the social conventions of our modern civilization and those of primitive barbaric peoples. In matters of ethics primitive peoples are not inferior to those who live in the centers of modern civilization. The rights of property are often strongly developed. I am told by those who have experience that the American Indian, unless corrupted by white influence, is inherently more honest in matters of property than any civilized people. An article of value left around among Indians in the Western Desert is far more likely to be recovered than the same article would be if it were left lying around in New York City. The emotional significance that we attach to the word "savage" is one of our own peculiar conceits. No doubt savages are often brutal, but I think we can scarcely argue that our modern civilization with its dope rings, murder squads, secret police, gas chambers, hydrogen bombs, or even with the knifing of innocent people in the streets of Los Angeles and New York possesses any great measure of superiority. Also I imagine that the marriage customs of most savages would be preferred by psychiatrists to the situation in Victorian England or in present-day Eire. In his mortuary activity modern man differs hardly at all from the men of thirty thousand years ago, a point already noted in the fourth chapter. In religion too I find little difference. Primitive man sees evidence of supernatural activities and of the existence of gods and devils in the origins of storm and drought and in the motions of the Sun and Moon. Modern man sees evidence of the existence of a supernatural power in the origin of the Universe. The framework is different, because our knowledge vastly excels that of primitive man, but the central concept is the same in the two cases. In art too I see no great measure of superiority between the works that adorn our art galleries and the paintings that primitive man was executing (under difficult physical conditions) on the rock walls of his caves some twenty thousand years ago. Indeed I see a considerable superiority in the latter over many productions that rejoice under the name of "modern art."

It is necessary to emphasize that I am not maintaining a complete social identity of modern society with the societies of ten thousand years ago, or even of twenty thousand years ago. What I am saying is that those social factors that do not relate to knowledge are essentially identical. But those that relate to knowledge are vastly different. The differences lie in transportation, communication, the availability of machines to replace human muscle power, medical services, great agricultural and industrial production, vast destructive powers. These are the altered components, not the emotional factors.

After this diversion I would like to go back to knowledge as a superstructure. What I have now to say is somewhat difficult to explain and may even be a little fantastic. It depends on the structure being something more than its parts. Suppose that each of the individual cells in our own bodies were to concern themselves with the problem of structure. They would notice that a human is compounded out of many of them. They would notice that an individual cell might die without impairing the general structure, that its place was often taken by a new cell. If moreover the cells were endowed with a conceit of themselves, they would surely argue that the totality of cells could not possess any consciousness that they themselves as individuals did not possess. And in this they would be entirely wrong, for the human possesses a consciousness that is not a consciousness possessed by individual cells. In short, the total human structure has properties that its individual components would not be immediately aware of.

Now let us scale up this little fantasy. Instead of taking cells as the individuals we take humans as the individuals. Instead of taking a human as the structure, we take the superstructure compounded out of humans. Does this superstructure possess a power and a consciousness of which we as the individual components are at best only dimly aware? I suspect that it does, and I suspect that it is this Thing that controls the destiny of the human species.

In my view human history is not so much a history of individuals as a history of the growth of The Thing. A not too farfetched analogy is given by the cooling of a gas. To begin with the particles of the gas act as separate individuals, except that occasionally one particle collides with another. This is the analogue of the early nomadic existence of Man. Then as the gas cools it happens that colliding particles do not always separate. They form together into little groups of which there may be a vast number in the whole gas. Here we have the beginning of a community existence, of the grouping of humans into small villages. Then with further cooling the small aggregations join together into drops of liquid—now we have the beginnings of an urban existence. Next the droplets mass together and a liquid is formed. The structure of the liquid is vastly more complicated than that of the original gas. The behavior of an individual is no longer independent of its neighbors, but it is not entirely controlled by them: a particle can move around, but it cannot move freely as it could when the material was gaseous.

The last step occurs when with further cooling the liquid freezes, and a solid is formed. Now the particles can no longer move around at all—they become completely controlled by the structure of which they are members. In the liquid and solid states we have the analogues of the fluid and rigid forms of civilization. The rise of modern civilization in Europe and North America during the last two or three centuries has been of an essentially fluid character. A man was obliged to behave reasonably in an understood way toward his neighbors, but a fair measure of individual freedom was permitted. Other civilizations have evolved to the solid state. Roman civilization had become pretty solidified by the time of its collapse. Chinese civilization in modern times collapsed before Western civilization largely because of its solidified character.

How fanciful is this? I suspect not at all. Indeed I imagine that a good deal of the mathematical analysis that is applicable to the association of particles in solids, liquids, and gases may turn out to be also applicable to the association of humans. The enormous historic changes of the last few thousand years, and even of the last few hundred years, have very much the appearance of what physicists call a co-operative phenomenon. A co-operative phenomenon is one in which to begin with a number of individuals change themselves in some particular. This does not have much effect on the whole group. Then if the proportion of changed individuals continues to grow, a quite critical point is reached. So long as the proportion remains below the critical value the properties of the whole group are not much changed. But as soon as the critical value is exceeded the whole group suddenly switches to the new property. The essence of a co-operative phenomenon is that the change of group behavior is not gradual, it does not change slowly as the number of individuals changes. Instead there is a sudden change at the critical value. Sudden shifts of public opinion have all the hallmarks of a co-operative phenomenon. On a much larger canvas the sudden emergence of civilization during the last five thousand years, and in particular the enormous development of the last five hundred years, when measured against the several hundred thousand years in which man pursued his nomadic existence, seem only explicable as a co-operative phenomenon.

VII.

A Biological Paradox Resolved

WE HAVE now built up a sufficient body of argument to attempt a resolution of an apparent biological paradox. Let us first consider the explanation sometimes given by biologists for the way in which living creatures change.

The explanation is based on a highly plausible assumption: that in every species heritable variations arise spontaneously from time to time, each variation being confined initially to one individual. It is then argued that some of the changes enable the individuals concerned to fit in better than their fellows with the external environment. The meaning of "fit in better" is perhaps expressed more clearly by the phrase "better able to reproduce their kind in the environment in question." Thus individuals possessing "beneficial" variations generate a larger proportion of surviving offspring than is normal for their species, and since the variations are assumed to be heritable the same characteristic is, on the average, passed on to the offspring, who in their turn reproduce more rapidly than the normal. In such a way, generation by generation, the "beneficial" variations are passed on to a larger and larger proportion of the species. So a species changes, and always in a manner that, in an unchanging environment, would increase the reproductive rate. This is just what is meant by saying that the species becomes "better adapted to the environment." It should be noted that "reproductive rate" is here used in the specialized sense of the offspring that themselves survive to the reproductive age. "Birth rate," on the other hand, includes offspring that die before reaching the reproductive age. It would be possible in two closely related species for one to have the higher birth rate and the other the higher reproductive rate.

It is interesting to notice that a quite erroneous conclusion has repeatedly been drawn from these ideas. Consider a species among the higher animals, and let a heritable variation arise that gives a particular male more than normal physical strength. This individual then gains control of an unusually large number of females, and hence increases his reproductive rate. The resulting offspring are, on the average, more than normally strong, and hence also have high reproductive rates; and so on. Hence the species gradually becomes physically stronger. The argument is so far perfectly sound. What is not sound, however, is the generalization of this special case into the statement that natural selection ensures the survival of the strong and promotes the extinction of the weak. A variation that enables a herbivorous animal to harmonize better with its surroundings often leads to a higher reproductive rate, since the animal in question is then less likely to be killed by its enemies. Here we have a variation that favors the "weak" and hinders the survival of the "strong." Or again, the development of a social instinct enables a group, even if it only contains the "weakest" members of a species, to overcome the "strongest" individual members. The development of the brain of man has enabled him not only to hold his own against much stronger members of the ape family, but through the invention of tools to reduce such creatures as the gorilla to comparative ineffectiveness. The terms "strong" and "weak" have no particular reference to natural selection.

We may also mention another erroneous idea that has achieved some currency. Noticing how well all plants and animals are adapted to their environment, it has been argued that there must be some deep inner purpose underlying the evolutionary process; that evolution is a means for putting some "grand plan of Nature" into operation. How nonsensical this notion is can be seen from the consideration that adaptation could immediately be destroyed by a gross change in the environment; for example, the adaptation of plants and animals living in the temperate zone would be largely destroyed by a sudden reversion to the conditions of an ice age. The situation is this: if the environment changes so slowly that evolutionary selection can readily keep pace, living creatures will always seem well adapted, no matter what the environment should become, within reasonable limits; if, on the other hand, the environment changes very rapidly, too rapidly for selection to keep step, there will be a notable absence of the high degree of adaptability that seems such a cause for wonder to some people.

After this preamble let us come now to the problem. The human species has changed vastly in its numbers and behavior during the last fifty thousand years—the number of humans has increased perhaps as much as five-thousandfold. How do we fit this great outburst into the evolutionary picture outlined above? Nothing daunted by this problem some geneticists have argued that changes of human behavior occur at the behest of changes in the individual. It has been argued that what has happened during the last fifty thousand years, even the great changes of the last five thousand years, are explicable in terms of changes in the human unit. It is very seriously to be doubted whether this is so. I doubt whether changes of the individual human have been at all appreciable during the last fifty thousand years. This is not to say that no changes at all occur in such an interval, but rather that such changes as have occurred are in no way commensurate with the extraordinary explosive outburst of humanity. And when the geneticist seeks to explain the history of the recent civilized era in terms of individual changes the case seems to me to become altogether ridiculous. The dilemma of orthodox biology is admitted by many biologists, who agree that no important evidence exists in support of the view that human development is a result of changes in the individual. The dilemma is that, according to orthodox biology, change must occur genetically (i.e., through the individual), and yet the evidence concerning humans is opposed to this view. Rather does it seem as if the most extraordinary development ever to occur among the animals has been brought about without any significant genetical change.

And this is just what I believe to be the case. Human history is an amazing story because it is a story of the gradual development of a structure built out of individuals, not through a change in the individuals themselves. A gas condenses into a liquid not through any change in the individual particles but through a developing interrelation of one particle with another. This I think is just what has happened to the human species. The change from the savage of a hundred thousand years ago to the writing of the Beethoven Sonatas is a consequence of the development of The Thing.

There is a sense in which the orthodox ideas of natural selection may be said to survive the present interpretation (although the purely genetical theory of change does not survive). It can be said that the potentiality for the building of a superstructure out of human units must lie within the units themselves. But this argument does not seem to me to have any useful application. We might as well say that human behavior is a manifestation of the properties of electrons, protons, and neutrons; and that the study of biology is really a side branch of fundamental physics.

It seems that a quite insufficient allowance has been made for structures built out of animal units. The human example shows how enormously important structure can be. It also shows that the development of a structure need not be an outcome of comprehensive genetical changes; a structure once it begins to control a species can apparently develop in its own right.

It is now time to say a little more about our repeated statement that a structure is something more than the units of which it is composed. We can gain a further insight into this by returning to our analogy of gases and liquids. The structural property that constitutes the liquid state is not the unique property of any one type of particle—there are a multitude of different substances all of which can form liquids. There are a multitude of cases where the structural property is the same, but the individual units are different. In a like manner there are many animals that possess superstructures—we have already mentioned bees and ants as notable cases.

The upshot of these remarks is that the structure built out of humans is not necessarily a uniquely human phenomenon. If other animals were to become controlled by The Thing, then I think it quite likely that the power and dominance that today we associate only with the human species would also become associated with other species. I could imagine that other species of mammals might become quite good at mathematics if they once got The Thing behind them. And I imagine that the views of birds on the subject of aerodynamics might be worth hearing.

It may be wondered why humanity has become organized into a formidable superstructure. Was this a matter of accident, or does the human unit possess properties that are specially suited to The Thing? Both, I think. Man's very slow start, his million years or so of food-gathering near the limits of survival would seem to confirm the lack of inevitability of human history. On the other hand, I do not think it can be denied that the human unit is well adapted to the formation of a superstructure. This is shown by the development of language. The establishment of effective communication between one individual and another undoubtedly represented the first step in the development of The Thing. The vital importance of communication has been much emphasized in recent years.

But at a deeper level the inherent structure of the human brain supplies the key to the matter. The design of the human brain, although not apparently differing in principle from the brains of other animals, is specially suited to the establishment of a superstructure. This is so crucial a point that it is worth while considering in detail in a separate chapter.

VIII.

What Is the Mind?

IN MY young days radio in the home was coming into vogue as a source of entertainment. We boys used to rate the quality of the various receivers in our village (we knew about them all) by the number of electronic tubes that they contained: "John Whittingham has got eight in his," we used to say in awe. It never occurred to us that our own bodies were pieces of electronic equipment with something like ten thousand million tubes in each of them.

The human tubes are usually spoken of as nerve cells, or more simply as neurons. They are mostly, although not entirely, located in the head, in the brain. A considerable number of electrical connections—nerve fibers—are attached to each neuron. These connections can be divided into two groups, input fibers and output fibers. The importance of the neuron lies in an ability to send an electrical impulse along its output fibers after it receives impulses along a sufficient number of input fibers. This is very similar to the way we use man-made tubes in an electronic calculator.

A few words are necessary about the meaning of the phrase "a sufficient number of input fibers." It seems that not all input fibers are of equal effect on the neuron to which they are attached; some are more effective in causing a "firing" of the neuron than others. The efficaciousness of an input fiber apparently depends on its mode of attachment to the neuron, on the "synaptic threshold" as it is sometimes called. And the synaptic threshold seems to be lowered with frequent use, so that the fiber in question becomes more effective in its ability to trigger off the neuron. It is apparently in this that the basis of memory and of learning lies.

Of course an ordinary electronic tube needs an external source of power for its operation—a battery for example. It may be wondered how the analogy with the neuron holds up here. How does the neuron derive its source of electric power? From chemicals supplied to it by the blood. The blood acts as a chemical battery.

Let us now consider the arrangement of neurons and nerve fibers in the head and body. We have spoken of the bulk of the neurons as being inside the head. A considerable fraction of these cerebral neurons are arranged in a highly convoluted sheet known as the cortex, the convolutions having the advantage that the sheet can be of a very considerable area and yet manage to fit inside the head. A man would need a vast pumpkin of a head to incorporate his cortex but for the convolutions, just as he would need a vast chest to hold his lungs if they were not also convoluted, and—not such a polite topic—a vast belly to hold his intestines.

There are also other centers of nervous activity located near the base of the brain. These centers, now incorporated into the general functioning of the human nervous system, may well be survivals from an earlier evolutionary stage; they may be primitive brains that existed long before the development of the cerebral cortex itself.

Next consider the input connections to the brain. These are derived from the so-called five senses, which consist of nerve cells appropriately stationed in the rest of the body, and which send their impulses along fibers to the brain. The sense of touch, for example, is made up of a very large number of sensory adapters—nerve cells—in the skin that are connected to the brain by a multitude of fibers. The connections are not sent up to the brain in a higgledy-piggledy manner, however. They go to the spinal column, where they form input fibers to groups of nerve cells resident in the spinal column: such groups of neurons may also be relics of a brain that operated in a distant evolutionary stage. Then from these nerve cells bundles of fibers, now sorted out into an orderly array, continue up the spinal column whence they eventually reach the cerebral cortex.

As with the sense of touch, the impulses from the other sensory adapters do not go immediately to the cortex. Impulses from the nerve cells in the eyes, for example, go to one of the low centers near the base of the brain, where some sorting process presumably takes place. Thence impulses are relayed to the part of the cortex at the back of the head.

When under normal conditions all five senses are operating, electric impulses reach the cortex from the eyes, ears, the smell adapters, from the touch adapters, and from adapters in the mouth. The nerves carrying all these impulses, besides being sorted into orderly bundles, are sent to separate parts of the cortex, each sensory adapter being allotted to its appropriate place.

Before we discuss further the brain activity resulting from this sensory input, it is desirable to say something about the output connections of the cortex. Output connections direct muscular behavior. The muscles of the legs are primarily controlled by impulses that travel from the brain along a bundle of fibers that go down the spinal column to a group of nerve cells, whence other nerve fibers carry the impulses to the various muscular tissues: an interruption in the downgoing fibers leads to a paralysis of the muscles in question, even though the brain and the muscles themselves may both be capable of perfect working.

We may also note that just as input connections from different sensory adapters are sent to different parts of the cortex, so different muscular controls come from different parts of the cortex; for instance speech is controlled by a certain region on the left side, damage to which can render a person incapable of speech.

We now reach a crucial question: what is the relation of the ingoing signals from the sensory adapters to the outgoing instructions to the muscles? Perhaps the best way to attack this question is to consider the method used by the brain to extract information from the sensory data. It would seem that the cells of the cortex, to which the sensory input fibers are directed, themselves possess output fibers that go to other, different cells of the cortex. These other cells occupy parts of the brain known as the "association areas." Now the connections to the association areas have the important property of mixing the sensory input. A cell in the association areas will usually possess connections not only to other cells in the same area but also to widely different parts of the cortex and in particular to the parts where the sensory inputs are first received: for example such a cell may have connections to cells that are receiving sense data from the ear, the eye, touch, etc. It would seem therefore that after mapping the sense data in an orderly way on various bits of the cortex, the next stage is one of greatly increased complexity in which the output fibers from these bits are mixed together in a more or less general fashion.

Next we notice that the output control to the muscles comes effectively from these same association areas. Accordingly we see that the orderly sensory input is not connected directly to the muscles; a general mixing process intervenes between the output control and the sensory data. This feature would seem to form the basis of human hehavior.

It may be emphasized that the nervous system of an animal possesses some properties that are fixed and some that are variable. The distinction is easily made: the fixed part is determined by the distribution of nerve cells and nerve fibers at the birth of the animal, while the variable part arises from the changes (e.g., of synaptic thresholds) that accompany the continued operation of the nervous system. The fixed part requires a baby to grow up in a characteristically human way and not with the mentality of a dog. It is very likely the fixed part that determines the essentials of our thinking, what we call logic. The fixed part is probably also responsible for the basis of our social behavior. On the other hand it is the variable part that enables us to acquire the language and customs of the particular community into which we happen to be born. Those features of behavior that arise from the fixed part may conveniently be termed "built in," or "wired in," or "instinctive" properties, and those features that arise from subsequent neurological modifications may be called "learned" properties. Behavior in an adult animal is a complex mixture of the two.

It may be asked: why bother with the variable properties? Why should we not be equipped with "built-in" properties only? The answer is, of course, that it is precisely the variable part of behavior that enables us to cope successfully with variations in our environment. If all our reactions were "wired in" we might be excellently adapted to one particular environment but favorable adaptation could immediately be destroyed by a sudden change of environment. Hence it is clear that the variable properties of the nervous system possess an important survival value. In this connection it may be noted that humans depend on learned properties more than any other animal.

A critic might say, "Granted that all these electrical processes occur in the brain, but where does the mind come in? What is it that actually experiences the seeing, hearing, feeling, and so forth?" The theory under review supplies unequivocal answers to these questions. The electrical activity of the brain is not scrutinized by an extraneous something called the "mind." It is quite wrong in my opinion to suppose that only when the mind comes into operation do we actually experience the sensations of seeing, hearing, thinking, etc. The present theory requires the electrical activity to actually be the sensation of seeing, hearing, thinking. . . . The "mind," if the word "mind" is to mean anything at all, must be taken as synonymous with the electrical activity itself.

For a valid objection to be raised against this point of view, the present theory would have to be shown inferior in its ability to explain human behavior to theories that claim an independent existence for the mind. So far from this having been demonstrated, the evidence is all in the opposite direction: the theory under brief mention in the present chapter has already achieved more in but a few years than the notion of an independent mind has been able to do in several millennia. Indeed without going into any details at all it is possible to deliver a shrewd blow at the notion of an independent mind. Thus assume for the moment the existence of an independent quality called "the mind" that in some way scrutinizes the electrical activity of the brain. Suppose also that it is through this scrutiny that the mind establishes consciousness. Then we ask: why does the scrutiny not take place directly from the mapping areas of the cortex? Why bother with the complication of the association areas, when all information concerning what is being seen, heard, smelt, tasted, and felt, is already available in the mapping areas? Such questions make it clear that on the hypothesis of an "independent mind" the existence of the association areas raises very considerable difficulties. On the present theory, however, the association areas are a vital necessity; "seeing" consists in analyzing current visual signals, possibly by a scanning technique, in terms of "memories" that have already been established in the association areas, the "memories" being simply neurological modifications caused by repeated experience. Thus "seeing" does not lie in the visual signals themselves, but in the analysis that takes place in the association areas. The analysis is the "seeing."

The well-known fact that we do not see everything that is being signaled by the eyes to the brain is immediately explicable in these terms. The reader may be "seeing" the words on this page but if he is stung at this instant by a wasp there will be a moment when he will cease to "see" the words, even though in that moment his eyes are still fixed on the page, and even though his eyes are still signaling to the brain in exactly the same way as they were before. In such a hypothetical case (I trust) very violent impulses are relayed through into the association areas from the sensory adapters in the neighborhood of the sting. These signals disturb and destroy the process of visual analysis. In a similar way any extraneous activity in the association areas tends to disrupt the analysis of visual signals. We may see either a great deal or very little according to circumstances quite extraneous to the optical information supplied by the eyes.

Now it would be possible to carry our present arguments a great deal further, to consider the learning process in more detail, for instance to consider learning through self-maintaining cycles, or to consider the difference between adult learning and infant learning. We could go on to build a theory of thinking. We might perhaps even build a plausible theory of the emotions of pain and pleasure in terms of associative and dissociative patterns of brain activity. We might explain neuroses, hysteria, and fits of rage in terms of self-amplifying brain circuits. But a detailed exposition of the ideas of neuropsychology is outside the scope of this book. Our aim in this chapter has been to establish new ideas that can usefully be related to the discussions of earlier chapters. This point has been reached and so, interesting as a further argument about the brain would be, it is high time we got back to the main stream of our argument.

We left The Thing rather abruptly at the end of Chapter VII. Let us now come back to it. Our aim, by way of concluding the present chapter, is to relate the structure of The Thing to the human brain.

The brain possesses a considerable measure of determined characteristics. An infant at birth is already "wired up" to a degree that makes it quite certain that it will grow up as a human, not as a dog or a gorilla. Prominent among the wired-in properties are the "emotions," "logic," a desire to associate with other members of the species, to communicate with others, to be well thought of. But the infant at birth does not possess any wired-in property to determine what particular sort of social relationship it will come to accept and demand in adult life. To the infant it is all one whether it is called on to accept the old nomadic existence of a hundred thousand years ago, or the caveman existence of twenty thousand years ago, or any of the civilized eras—Mesopotamian, Greek, Roman, modern. In short, the "wired-in" properties decide that the infant shall be a human, but they do not dictate what sort of human.

The degree of variability that we find in human social behavior is achieved by the learning process. The learning process acts as a coupling device whereby we can adjust ourselves to a wide variety of social conditions. But the coupling can be used really effectively only once. Once we have adapted ourselves to a particular language and society, the free coupling no longer exists any more. What we have learned becomes the "right" way to speak and behave, what we can no longer learn becomes "wrong" and must be opposed, to the death if need be.

It is just this initial free coupling that allows human society to change without the basic human units changing. It is just this free coupling that has allowed The Thing to gain its ascendancy over us. Yet I do not think that The Thing necessarily had much to do with the evolutionary development that led to our becoming equipped with free coupling. Even if we think of humans existing as single units, without any appreciable superstructure, the possession of a free coupling would have great biological survival value.

Suppose you were designing an animal. Reckoning that your design would have to cope with an environment that might change quite rapidly, you would evidently have to provide for rapid changes in your animal. If you allowed your basic units —the individual animals at birth—to change too quickly by the heritable processes studied by biologists, your animal would lack natural stability. It would change of its own accord too readily, even when there were no changes of environment. The only hope then of giving quick adjustment to environmental changes, together with adequate stability, would be to develop free coupling. This overcomes the dilemma. It allows behavior to change without the animal changing in any basic way (i.e., from what it was at birth). Thus we see, quite apart from any question of superstructure, how it is of great advantage to possess the measure of freedom implied by the learning process in Man. Other animals also learn, but not to the degree that Man does. Our measure of adaptability is the greatest, and I think it is precisely because of this that The Thing has got hold of us, for the free coupling enables us to adapt ourselves to social situations that are not specifically human—i.e., not dictated by the human wired-in properties.

In this we reach a conclusion that has been pending since the earliest chapters. When we were discussing the pros and cons of the communist issue we traced the detestation of communists to an almost unformed fear that it is the communists who are responsible for a general social malaise, of which I think we are all aware whether consciously or not. This view is so ludicrous that it would be a matter for laughter if it were not likely to lead to such serious consequences. The communists, especially the Russian communists, are naïve people who believe that they hold the key to Man's future. Their confidence in this respect is gained from the industrial expansion now taking place in Russia. It is a confidence entirely analogous in its origin to that of the nineteenth-century Englishman, or to that of the American of two or three decades ago. What the Russians have still to perceive is that while now they are having their fun, later they will have to pay for it. We on the other hand have had our fun and are already paying for it.

This book has a design consisting of two main cycles of argument. We have been following the first of these throughout all that has gone before. We have been tracing the origin of a present sense of social uneasiness. We started the Communist–Anti-Communist issue, not because our basic troubles really lie there, but because it is often said that they do. Then we followed the argument on increasingly detailed levels—taking in a historical survey meanwhile—until we were led to the concept of a human superstructure, which I have referred to as The Thing. The superstructure although it is compounded out of human units is something more than human in its characteristics. It is able to impress on us patterns of behavior that bear little relation to our innermost natures (which I have referred to unromantically as our "wired-in" properties). And it is this sense of being compressed into an alien mold that causes our present-day sense of unrest. It is this I think that lies at the root of our unformed fears. The symptoms of the case show themselves in multifarious ways whenever we speak about the "pressure" of modern life.

The second cycle of the book follows on naturally from the first: having recognized the symptoms of the disease we must go on to consider the possibilities of a cure. This we shall do in later chapters. For the present however I am going to take advantage of a breathing space between the two cycles to consider certain matters that fit neatly into neither cycle but which have some relevance to both. So the next chapter will fill in a pause between the two main sections of argument.

IX.

The Relationship of Individual and Community

WE HAVE already said that the behavior of an adult is only partly determined by the wired-in properties possessed at birth. Behavior is also much dependent on learning, on what we call "experience of the world." Our experience of the world is of two sorts, purely physical experience and experience that we acquire from our relations with other people. There is a notable difference between these two categories. One is highly relative, the other is not. Let us consider purely physical experience first.

The physical characteristics of the external world are the same for all individuals. We accordingly find a general universality in the concepts that come under this class; for example, all people with sight develop the same ideas about the shapes of objects, about distances and about the geometrical nature of space: no one yet seems to have thought of talking about marxist shapes or about capitalistic distance.

The situation is quite different for those concepts that are learned through the medium of other humans. Here an enormous degree of arbitrariness arises. The particular language that we learn in childhood is an example of this arbitrariness. Arbitrary standards of judgment pervade our general thinking to a much greater extent than is generally realized. An individual seems normal in appearance to us when his physical characteristics—the color of his skin, the length of his nose, the width between the eyes, the texture of the hair—agree with what we are used to in our own particular community. Beauty in a woman is determined by extreme normality of feature. I am told that there is a simple way of proving this. Under identical conditions of lighting, exposure time, etc., take photographs of about a score of girls chosen from the community in question but otherwise at random. Instead of printing the negatives separately let them be superimposed to produce a composite picture. What then emerges, if the blending is carefully done, will be adjudged a typical pretty girl. Moreover let the experiment be repeated with a different score of girls. Then the second composite photograph will be found to bear a remarkable likeness to the first. This arises from the blending of negatives which gives an averaging whereby the long-faced is canceled against the short-faced, the wide-eyed against the narrow-eyed, the long-nosed against the short-nosed, the large-mouthed against the small-mouthed, and so on. In the composite photograph only the average characteristic shows through. We see therefore that the receipt for feminine beauty is ordinariness, but in an uncommon degree: beauty is lost as soon as one important feature differs appreciably from the average for the community.

These remarks have interest in showing why standards of beauty can differ so markedly between different communities. They also suggest a mechanism whereby a community tends to maintain its physical appearance. Thus since by and large beautiful women are most attractive to men, there is an immediate selective factor favoring the preservation of the average characteristics. One should be careful, however, not to interpret this as a deep reason underlying our judgment of feminine beauty. Rather would it seem that beauty corresponds simply to what we are used to. This can apparently be varied in a more or less arbitrary manner. Thus the frequent showing of American films to colored peoples has apparently swung standards of beauty away from the normal and toward the American standard. Similarly a white man brought up entirely among Negroes judges beauty in the Negroid way rather than on the standard of his own people.

To forestall criticism it should be emphasized that the above remarks refer to shape not to color. It is somewhat curious that while normality is used to measure beauty of shape, beauty of color is sometimes enhanced by a deviation from the ordinary. Blue eyes and dark hair are generally thought more noteworthy than the usual combination of blue eyes and light hair; the blonde is usually thought more attractive when she is in the company of brunettes. There is of course a limit to the variations of coloration that can be tolerated; for example red eyes and black teeth are not thought attractive.

Probably an analysis of other forms of beauty—beauty in sound, beauty of art, beauty of landscape—would reveal a multitude of examples of arbitrary standards of judgment. The object of the present discussion is not, however, to stress the relative quality of the notion of beauty, but to bring out the relative nature of nearly all our social conventions. Every community has its own rules of behavior. Perhaps it may sound a little cynical, but I suspect that if a particular action happens to fit in with the rules of our own community we describe it as a right, or a moral, or a just action; and the other way round if the rules are violated: then we say that the action is wrong, unjust, or evil. This means that a moral code is something relative to the community in question. It also means that a discussion based on moral issues is scarcely likely to be successful in settling an argument between different communities with different rules of behavior—a conclusion amply borne out by the facts of history.

These views are also supported by many current examples. It will be sufficient to consider a few of the more interesting illustrations. Patriotism is an obvious case of relativity of outlook: the Englishman fights for England because he feels that it is "right" for him to do so; and the Russian fights for the U.S.S.R. on a like basis. The origin of such beliefs lies, of course, in social learning. Indeed if the Russian and the Englishman were called on to fight each other, each would seek to justify himself with precisely the claim that his own society possesses the virtues of goodness and that the opposing society was corrupt and evil. A demand for factual proof would in each case lead, not to proof, but to irritation.

"Whoever heard of anybody being asked to prove anything so obvious?" each would exclaim. The irony is that if the two had been swapped at birth, they would have behaved similarly, except that all their social concepts would have been the other way round.

In marriage customs there are especially wide variations from one community to another. To some people monogamy seems a natural practice, to some polygamy, and to still others, polyandry. In some societies bastardy is frowned on, in others a man and woman do not marry until after the first child is born to them.

In capitalist countries offenses against bureaucracy are punished but carry no social stigma. In communist countries similar offenses are swollen up (as we should say) into offenses against the State itself, whence they are regarded as heinous crimes to be set on a par with robbery and murder. Indeed the whole field of "justice" has a very considerable relativity of point of view.

On occasions this would seem to be understood by lawyers. Lawyers show notable insight in preferring to base practical justice on precedent, instead of trying to build a logical legal system. Justice requires offenses against certain canons of social behavior to be punished. Since the canons of behavior are often of a quite arbitrary character it is clear that no sound procedure other than precedent can be found. If it be asked why an offense against an arbitrary code of behavior should be punishable at all, the answer is that a community must organize itself on some set of rules, which however relative their character must be obeyed if a fair degree of harmony is to be achieved. It is immaterial whether a community chooses to drive its automobiles on the right or the left side of the highway, but it must choose one side or the other! The essence of the matter is not which rules we adopt, but that having arrived at a particular set of rules we should stick to them in order that social cohesion be maintained. An individual who finds distasteful the rules of the community in which he happens to live should forthwith quit that community and seek some other where the rules are more to his liking. If he does not do so, and if he insists on breaking the rules that seem to him objectionable, then he will only have himself to blame if punishment ensues.

It is curious that while lawyers would seem to have a clear appreciation of the advantages of the system of precedent, the legal mind seems to be plagued by a strange inconsistency of thought. Although in practice concessions are made to the relative quality of justice, one gets the impression from reading their pronouncements that most lawyers at bottom hold the concept of a clear, shining, absolute standard of justice.

Only a belief in an absolute "right" could have led to the singular concept of "international law." A system of law is only possible in a community that possesses both a uniform set of conventions and a means for enforcing them. The procedure of "international law" possesses neither of these qualifications. Accordingly it is hardly surprising that the effect of "international law" in the postwar world has been quite negligible. Whatever arguments may be urged in its favor, "international law" has not been able to exercise a stabilizing effect on the world at a time when a stabilizing effect is urgently needed, and has hence failed to supply serious evidence of its value. Even in such a comparatively minor matter, the International Court at The Hague was obliged to declare the recent quarrel

H

between Persia and Great Britain as outside its jurisdiction. Of course the Court had no jurisdiction, since Persia did not accept the conventions that would allow "international law" to operate, and the International Court did not possess the power to enforce them.

It might be as well at this stage to give some attention to a critic who might argue thus: "There must be some conventions that are universal to all societies, and insofar as universal conventions exist, so there must be an absolute sense of justice and of right and wrong." Without wishing to argue that there are no such conventions, I would point out that it is not easy to give examples. It might be thought that murder would always be in violation of social conventions but this is not so. In the past murder was an everyday occurrence in Sicily; and what we should certainly describe as murder, namely female infanticide, has been, and is, practiced as a matter of social policy by various peoples—for example by the Eskimos. Even the avoidance of incest, although it comes near it, is not quite a universal convention; for example incest was practiced as a matter of policy by the Egyptian Pharaohs. Indeed incest is likely to occur whenever a particular family comes to hold the belief that it possesses some special admirable quality that sets its members apart from the rest of the community. The quite extraordinary variations of human social behavior revealed by anthropological studies will make it very difficult for our critic to maintain his argument.

In contrast to many adults, my small nephew of eight had no difficulty in perceiving the relativity of his own outlook when he wrote the following essay:

My Favorite Hobby

My favorite hobby is boxing
becaes I am very intrestib
in it. I have basht many
boys in. they are very tuf to.
I have herd that a man
had been noct-out and he
won the mach on points.
I am very tuf at times.
I am very good at boxing.
I thick boxing is good very
very good. I box with my
father some times. Boxing
is a good hobby if you
loock at it my way. You
have to be tuf in boxing.
the boxes are very tuf.
Boxing is very good I
thick it is very very
very good bon't you?
                    the end.   W.A.

Perhaps the oddest thing about social relationships is the strength with which we hold the arbitrary conventions of our own group. In contrast the conventions of science and mathematics are adopted entirely without emotion; they are viewed simply as conveniences that can be changed at any time. By the phrase "without emotion" we mean that a change of convention does not produce any serious disruption of our scientific thinking. A change of social convention, on the other hand, is almost always associated with emotional stress.

The explanation would seem to lie in an important wired-in property of the human brain. In each of us there would seem to be an overwhelming desire to be thought well of by our fellow creatures. Disapproval of our actions by a single individual, especially by a close relative or friend, is sufficient to produce a fair degree of mental disintegration; an expression of disapproval by the whole of the community in which one lives induces a shattering disturbance. The effect is neurologically analogous to a sudden physical change that leaves one "rooted to the spot in terror"; that is to say, the normal brain patterns are disrupted to such an extent that purposive action is lost. An individual subjected to widespread censure expresses himself by saying that he has "nobody to turn to," or that he has "no purpose left in life." So decisive and final is the whole affair that he may well find it impossible to rebuild his shattered mental state. Instead of trying to do so he may prefer to transfer himself to an entirely different community, even though this means learning from scratch an entirely new system of social conventions. The object of such a change is to enable the unfortunate victim to become once again a normal, or almost normal, member of *some* society.

It should be emphasized that I am not referring here to cases of physical compulsion: the driving force comes not from outside but from within. Nor does it seem that our desire for the approval of our fellows, our desire to "fit in," is a learned response. We have apparently to do with a wired-in property of the brain. It is on this basis that all social behaviorism seems to be built; it is indeed this wired-in property that has made Man into a social animal. Perhaps we should consider a few examples. Let us begin with the case of "conformity." Conformity requires a person to fit in with even the minor social conventions of his own society. Conformity is a well-known feature of modern American life. Indeed conformity in America now runs down to such trivial levels that many Americans are beginning to regard it with a sense of irritation. This is an instance of a clash arising between Man's social sense and his other faculties, in the conformity case most often with the logical faculties.

Another such clash arises in the phenomena of "conscience" and "duty." It is not uncommon for a man's brain to be activated by two mutually inconsistent patterns, one being connected with what we usually describe as a "personal advantage," the other with an important social convention. Should the social convention happen to be strong enough to suppress the personal interest, we say on some occasions that the individual in question is "doing his duty" and on other occasions that he is obeying "the voice of conscience." Which case is which depends on whether or not the rest of the community knows of the existence of the mental conflict. If it does, we say that the man is "doing his duty"; if it does not, we say that he is "obeying the voice of conscience." Acting according to conscience is a gratuitous obedience to social convention. Conscience has often been described as an absolute "God-given" quality: there is a sense in which this statement is valid, for obedience to social convention would appear to be the special wired-in property that makes Man a social animal. In contrast, the conventions that conscience causes us to obey can be quite arbitrary, and on a rational basis may indeed be quite absurd.

It has already been mentioned that obedience to social conventions is intertwined with the desire to be thought well of by one's fellows. The latter factor is probably primary: we obey social conventions because of an overriding desire to secure popular approval and to avoid general opprobrium. Indeed the desire to be well thought of underlies most of our social actions; for example, it supplies the driving force that determines a child's social learning, and probably an adult's too. This is often shown by the development of a young man's career, which frequently consists of a sort of shuffling process that continues by trial and error until a suitable niche is found in society. While the shuffling is going on a fair degree of mental unrest is manifest. The unrest disappears as soon as the individual manages to fit himself into the community in a satisfactory way.

The unrest just mentioned often starts in early adolescence, especially in the male. Indeed this type of disturbance is at least as much a cause of the general turbulence of adolescence as the sexual issues so much stressed by Freudian psychologists. It is commonplace for a young man to come to regard himself as an entire social misfit. When this happens some such process as the following would seem to occur in the brain: "If I am a misfit, a failure, if I can never manage to pull my weight, why then should I bother what people think about me? Why should I bother with all the various social conventions, conventions which are damned silly anyway?"

In short, when a young man feels he is an outcast he tends

to become a social rebel: this I think is the real reason why the young are less conventional than the old. The notion that crabbed age is conventional and raw youth unconventional is scarcely valid in any deep sense; experience in this respect is explicable quite simply on the basis that a much higher proportion of older people have managed to find secure places in society for themselves: reverse the situation, make youth secure and age insecure, and it is likely that the older people would then be the ones to become dissatisfied with the social conventions. Some support for this view is given by the fact that during childhood, while they are still surrounded by the security of the family, children are the most conventional of creatures.

Now what happens, it may be asked, to the adolescent who begins by feeling a misfit and who goes on to become an actual misfit? What happens to the person who never finds his niche, who becomes utterly convinced that society has no use for him? The answer is that such a person either suffers entire mental degeneration or he comes to join the criminal classes. Whereas the majority who manage to find places in the social structure develop a strong determination to uphold the conventions, the minority who find themselves, or who consider themselves, to be social outcasts develop a desire to break the conventions, or at any rate to break the less strongly held conventions. This is the first step toward criminality. The second step occurs when a person in such a state of mind comes into contact with actual criminals. He then discovers a new social group with which he is able to fit in readily: the qualification for being a wanted member of the criminal class is simply an enmity against the main body of society. This second step is probably decisive in the production of a criminal.

There are some who maintain that criminals are born. I doubt this. A simple receipt can be given for the production of criminals. Take children away from security at an early age, thereby forcing them before their time to seek a place in society. The proportion who are unsuccessful will develop in the manner outlined above, and these it will be who inevitably drift toward the criminal class. An equally simple receipt can be given for curing criminals: persuade them that they are indeed wanted members of the larger society. Punishment is quite useless as a cure. Incarceration in jail does, it is true, put a criminal out of harm's way but it is in no sense a cure, as the police are fully aware. The present prescription, it must be admitted, is not easy to carry out. It would be quite useless to read a criminal a lecture in which he was told that of course the community appreciated his existence: it would be useless simply saying that a place in society was available to him. The important thing would be to convince him that this was the case. To provide real conviction some practical evidence would have to be supplied. Training a criminal to do a useful job, while undoubtedly helpful in providing him with the means for taking up a normal place in society, is not itself sufficient. It would be necessary to specify the way in which the criminal could in fact acquire a proper social dignity. Difficult as it would be to succeed in this, it seems that a really serious effort in this direction is worth making. The extent of the effort that should be made can be estimated in financial terms, since it is evidently worth spending at least as much on cure as we are at present spending on incarceration.

THE RIGIDITY OF SOCIAL CONVENTIONS

It may be that some slight retreat from the position taken up above would prove necessary on a further analysis. In fairness to an opponent of the relativity of ethics I would agree that there is no complete arbitrariness in our adopted conventions. Many of our conventions, particularly the strong conventions, have a basis in utility. We spoke of the arbitrary quality of the patriotism of the Englishman and the Russian. But patriotism is not arbitrary in the sense that both the Englishman and the Russian are patriotic. Arbitrariness enters in deciding which side a man will support—that depends where on the Earth's surface he is born—but there is no arbitrariness in the sense that he will support one or other of the two sides. Such cases of a lack of relativity occur when a social convention has a survival value to the community that adopts it. The survival value of patriotism is an obvious example. Notice that I am not asserting that communities deliberately adopt rules of behavior that have a survival value but rather that those communities that do so—probably by chance—are the communities that survive. So the concession to a lack of relativity is not very great.

The key to what I want to say in this last part of the present chapter lies in the previous paragraph, in the remark that conventions with survival value only come to be adopted by chance, not by deliberate design. How much better it would be for a community if it were otherwise, if it were possible to recognize improvements in our rules of behavior and act accordingly. But I suspect that this can never be done because of the way that already existing rules interfere with the acceptance of new rules. This is a theme that I would like to develop a little, taking two types of community into consideration—first the totalitarian communities like Fascist Italy, Communist Russia, or Nazi Germany; second the democracies like Britain and the United States.

So let us consider whether any effective control over social evolution can be exercised by the so-called strong governments. The leaders of a totalitarian state have highly effective methods for indoctrinating their people with any specific belief, this being done partly by ceaseless propaganda and partly by the ruthless suppression of any alternative belief. At first sight one might suppose that under such conditions the beliefs of a people could be readily changed; surely here is the answer to the problem of keeping beliefs in step with changing circumstances; surely this is the way for evolution to take place in a controlled manner. These conclusions are entirely in error, however. Curiously enough states with this sort of government, so far from being capable of a controlled evolution, are entirely static in character. The fallacy in the strong government argument lies in the implicit assumption that the leaders arrive at appropriate new beliefs as they become necessary. To see that this is not so, let us consider in some detail how leaders come to power and where they themselves get their beliefs from.

Suppose that we have a set of established leaders possessing a particular outlook. Should the state be totalitarian the beliefs of the leaders will become heavily imposed on the whole population. Now since political pomp cannot combat death, there must be replenishments among the leaders from time to time; and—here is the crucial point—in the usual course of events the new recruits come from the people. It follows therefore that new leaders must hold the same ideas as the old, much more so in a totalitarian state than in a society with a loosely knit organization and where free speech is tolerated. This conclusion is strengthened by the circumstance that those young men who conform most strenuously to the views of the leaders are most likely to be themselves chosen as the new leaders. Accordingly we see that a totalitarian society is utterly unable to evolve. The first group of leaders determine the views of the people; the views of the people determine the views of the next group of leaders; the next group of leaders continue to control the views of the people; and so it goes on ad infinitum—or more precisely until changes of circumstance bring the community to an entire collapse.

These remarks serve to emphasize a point that is usually not given sufficient attention. We hear a great deal about the people of a state being subjected to seductive propaganda but we hear very little about how the leaders of the state come to hold the ideas that are being indoctrinated. The answer is very simple. Except perhaps under very rare circumstances, the leaders of a society hold views that correspond to the average beliefs of the people in general: otherwise the leaders would not have gained the support that was necessary for them to have become the leaders. This is certainly true in a democratic society, and it is largely true of the party that finally gains power in the sort of political free-for-all that follows a social revolution. Minority opinion can obtain overriding power only when the majority of the people have no clear-cut views to put forward; this was the situation for example in Russia at the time of the Communist revolution. Even in such cases the successful minority is usually the largest of the sections that happens to know what they want, so that in a sense the successful minority may be said to represent the predominant opinion.

A critic might argue thus: "Consider a tyrant who robs and beats his subjects, and who ravishes any woman that happens to take his fancy. Do the actions of such a tyrant accord with majority opinion?" In answer I would say that whenever tyrannical behavior is persistent it must reflect majority opinion. This does not mean that a robbed man or a ravished woman expresses pleasure at the treatment received. It means that the common man would behave in the same way if he happened to be in the tyrant's shoes. In short, tyrannical behavior is permitted by a community if, and only if, the behavior seems normal to the majority. Indeed properly speaking there can be no such thing as a firmly established oppressive government. A government either behaves in a manner that seems more or less normal to the people or else the government falls; and this applies even in the totalitarian state. We are often told that the people in a totalitarian state are kept in abeyance by the secret police. It is not too strong to say that this view is plain rubbish. Secret police may be able to suppress the hostility of a comparatively small minority, but secret police are quite

powerless to suppress the determined hostility of the majority
—it is doubtful whether during the late war the German Gestapo on its own account could have held Europe in subjection
for a single day: German domination was then based, not on
secret police, but on the major strength of the German army.

Leaving this diversion on tyranny, we now return to the
main discussion. A society can alter its beliefs only if there is
some process whereby the majority of the people can alter their
beliefs freely and spontaneously, since only in this way can the
views of the leaders be changed. No such process exists at all
in the totalitarian state. In a democracy such a process exists
in theory, but does not work well in practice. Under democratic conditions it is possible for the individual to express himself as opposed to a particular belief and for him to try to
persuade others of his point of view by talking and by writing.
It is also possible for him to advocate some new belief. In a
democratic country a process accordingly exists whereby the
ideas of the majority can be changed. But on a more detailed
examination the process is found not so effective as it may
appear at first sight. Nevertheless a democratic society may
validly be regarded as better able than a totalitarian state to
adapt itself to changes of circumstance.

In a democratic society the individual who attacks a firmly
held belief is subjected to severe social pressure, if not to physical suppression. Nor is it easy to see how this situation can be
changed since the stability of a community would be threatened if its rules of behavior could be too easily challenged. We
must always remember that the majority of new ideas, like the
majority of genetical changes in a species, are not useful and

would be actively harmful if they came to be adopted. It is therefore very necessary that they should be suppressed. How then do we distinguish the minority of useful ideas from the majority of useless ones? Herein lies the evolutionary dilemma that faces the democracies, for evolution is vitally dependent on the useful minority of new beliefs and ideas. The evolution of our democratic communities is dependent on picking out a few gems from a vast pile of rubble. To discontinue the search because the gems are not easily found is to court the certain disaster that must sooner or later overtake a fossilized society. To confuse every bit of rubble with a precious stone would be equally foolish. The dilemma is still unsolved.

X.

The Evolution of Humanity

IT MIGHT seem from what has just been said that humanity cannot evolve, a palpably erroneous conclusion as the historical record shows. Yet how shall we reconcile the manifest tendency of human communities to fossilize themselves in accordance with a set of established conventions with the enormous development of Man during the last ten thousand years? The answer to this question lies in the existence of a multiplicity of communities with varying conventions. We are to think here of the conventions adopted by a particular community as more or less a matter of chance. Indeed it is just because of the chance element that variations occur from one community to another.

Now it will happen in a multiplicity of communities that a select few, or perhaps even a solitary community, possesses conventions that happen to promote the development of knowledge to a greater degree than the rest. We may express this by saying that one (or a few) of the communities happens to be better in tune with The Thing. Observe now what The Thing does for this community. It promotes the growth and expansion of the community (*vide* the rise of the Greeks). A time comes when the community becomes so large and powerful that it is able to impress itself on weaker communities, and also on larger fossilized communities. This it seems to do in two different ways. The new vigorous community defeats a larger fossilized community by war. Usually being roundly defeated in war serves to break up the conventions of the fossilized community thereby giving its people a new start (although sometimes the defeat is so complete that no fresh start is possible, as in the case of the Roman defeat of Carthage). The case for the weaker communities is different. These, being weak, must perforce accept the dictates of the vigorous expanding community. This passivity is important, as we shall soon see.

Because a weaker community is no immediate threat to the expanding community the weak group (especially if it is geographically rather distant) is not forced into the conventional pattern of the expanding community. So long as the weak community allows itself to be exploited in the commercial sense it is often allowed to proceed as it wills. And in this lies the ultimate downfall of the expanding community. For what the weak group does is to accept those features of the culture of the powerful group that relate to The Thing, but nothing else. Stated differently, the weak accept the technology of the strong but not their moral and ethical conventions. We can see this actually in operation in the world today. The colored peoples are accepting wholeheartedly the white man's technology, but they are not accepting in any real degree the rest of the white man's culture. Indeed the white man is often actively despised for the rest of his culture.

The expanding community thus sows the seeds of its own destruction. As it proceeds along the path toward fossilization it gives away the secrets of its own success to others. Sooner or later one of the weaker communities will chance on a social organization that serves the ends of The Thing even better than its master. This particular community then starts to expand and the cycle is repeated.

All this expresses in a different language the civilization cycle discussed in an earlier chapter. It will be recalled that overpopulation was regarded as an important feature of the civilization cycle and it may therefore be wondered where overpopulation enters the present argument. It enters in the promotion of fossilization. A hitherto vigorous expanding population rapidly becomes fossilized when it becomes overpopulated. It is not difficult to trace the reason for this. A community is overpopulated when it has to support more nonproductive people than its productive capacities warrant. In the ancient civilizations production was synonymous with food production. In our modern civilization food production cannot be separated from industrial production, but overpopulation still implies an overrunning of food profits. When a harmful excess of nonproductive people arises these people feel it imperative to justify their existence. Since this cannot be done on any rational basis it has to be done by inventing a mass of conventional procedures that can only be punctiliously carried out with the aid of their services. To make this device effective it is essential that the conventional procedures

I

shall come to be esteemed more highly than actual food production itself. In this way the community saddles itself with a host of useless conventions and it comes to accept a wholly false sense of values. It becomes fossilized. In the last century the British were a vigorous expanding community. Today they are a fossilized overpopulated community with a distorted sense of values. For instance there is scarcely a nation in the world to which food production is so important. Yet those who work on the land in Britain are the poorest paid of all workers. A similar fate awaits the United States, and will (I feel safe in predicting) happen unless Americans appreciate the danger and take steps in time to meet it.

Coming back now to our main argument, we can summarize all that has been said in terms of a biological analogy. We discussed in an earlier chapter the operation of natural selection as it affects the biological development of the individual animal. There is also a natural selection of groups of individuals that proceeds quite independently of any change in the individual, and which can happen in a period that is much shorter than the time required to produce an appreciable change in the individual. This group evolution applies to all gregarious animals, and it applies with exceptional force to humans. Natural selection in the Darwinian sense refers to individuals *in* an environment—perhaps *plus* an environment would be better. To apply our analogy we must therefore have groups of humans—communities—plus an environment. Now what is the environment that controls the evolution of Man in the group sense? It is just "The Thing," itself. Evolution takes place in such a way that The Thing extends its scope and its power. The Thing progresses. The human individual does not progress except insofar as he is a component of The Thing. History is not the record of the development of human individuals (as in our egoism we like to imagine), but of the development of The Thing. This development has been achieved by the rise and fall of a whole multitude of communities each of which has contributed in some degree. The use of war as a means of breaking up fossilized, overrigid communities is an essential feature of the process. So far, The Thing has been well served by war. Mars has had a high rank among the gods.

XI.

Crisis in the Modern World:
The First Problem

THE FULL depth of the present world crisis lies immediately before us. The age-old selection of human communities has broken down. The Thing has evolved to such a degree that it can no longer be served by war. War can no longer establish rising vigorous communities in place of fossilized communities. War in the future must break up all communities. In precise terms, it is the unleashing of nuclear energy that has brought about the changed situation. Knowledge as represented by The Thing, in this case physical knowledge, has produced the necessity for a world-wide change in the organization of human civilization. The Thing can now only develop further in a single-power world. It cannot develop as it did in the past in a multipower world.

What is going to happen? For my own part I think we can be sure that The Thing is going to have its own way. It has always had its own way in the past and it is more than likely to go on having it in the future. If The Thing demands a single-power world then we shall get a single-power world, whether we like it or not. Where we do have a choice however is in the manner in which we shall get our single-power world, what degree of pain we shall suffer in getting there. If we (and I mean Russians here as well as everybody else) allow ourselves to slip smoothly into a one-power world, the transition will be achieved with the minimum of discomfort. If on the other hand we insist on our right to national sovereignties, on our right to build a multipower world we shall be punished with severity. World wars will then continue to break up our social organization until at length, either voluntarily or by chance, we arrive at a single-power world. This I think is the extent of our choice.

There are some who say that the hydrogen bomb has made further wars impossible. These people say that mankind has such a horror of death that even in a multipower world we shall never again take steps that lead to war. The strength of this argument can be evaluated by a drive along a crowded highway. We are horrified by the sight of an accident. In our imagination we see our own car lying battered by the roadside, our own self as the corpse beneath the sheet. Yes, but how are we driving twenty miles farther down the road? And does the thought of yesterday's accident instill much caution into us today? Man has a horror of the death that he sees with his own eyes, but remote death has little sting. And perhaps it is as well that it should be so, otherwise we should be harrowed out of existence.

In any case everybody recognizes that at root this argument is an absurdity: for if we really took it seriously then should not Nobel Peace Prizes all be awarded in the future to the inventors of new and more formidable methods of mass slaughter?

I am not a naturally melancholy or pessimistic person, yet I suffer mental depression once daily when I read the morning newspapers. Mercifully the depression on some days is less severe than on others. What it is that works the mischief (in my case) is the daily insistence that Man is determined to learn his lesson the hard way, the insistence that Man is determined to build a multipower world on the oldest of old patterns. Today we have a two-power world, the powers being of course the U.S. and the U.S.S.R. It is perhaps because a two-power world is the next best thing to a one-power world that we have just managed to prevent world war during the last five or six years. But this advantageous situation is soon to become a thing of the past. Russia is insisting on the emergence of China as a world power, and the United States is insisting that Western Europe, with Germany in the lead, shall make up a dubious quartet. The chance of avoiding war in a four-power world can I think be written off as negligible; the possibilities of disagreements flaring into war will then become too numerous for our present limping diplomacy to control.

What can be done about this most urgent situation? Nothing I fear by ordinary political methods. Voting in one set of politicians rather than another at an election can have no effect at all. In this matter the political parties, whether Democrat or Republican in the United States, or Labour or Conservative in Britain, have no real difference between them. The democratic process in the West, the democratic process of which we affect to be so proud, has been reduced to a choice between near identities. However our votes are cast at the next election we shall get very nearly the same thing, one or other of two identical twins. We shall get policies that belong to an outdated past. We shall get policies that have no sensible chance of working in the present-day world.

Who is to blame for this mockery of democracy? Not the politicians but we ourselves. It is we, the people, who refuse to take democracy seriously. We regard democracy as a luxury to which we have a birthright, instead of seeing in democracy something that has to be worked for and paid for. We shall only have a real democracy when every man regards it as a serious duty to think about world affairs, to discuss them with his neighbors, and to acquaint his political representatives in no uncertain terms of his conclusions when he reaches them. A man regards it as natural to provide financially for his family. Is it not important that he should also take any steps he can to ensure the physical safety of his family? Instead we are content that our democratic duties should be confined to voting once every two or three years, voting to decide whether we shall be ruled by Tweedledum or by Tweedledee. In these circumstances it is a matter for astonishment that we get as good government as we do.

XII.

Population: The Second Problem[*]

LET US suppose that a near miracle comes about. Let us suppose that the peoples of the world waken to their responsibilities in time, and that a smooth transition to a single-power world is achieved. Do we then sink back into lethargy? By no means, for there are other equally grave problems to be tackled. One of them, the one to be discussed in this chapter, is contained in Figure 2, which shows how the world's population has swollen over the ages. The problem is manifest from the steep climb of the curve. Stated tersely, the world's population is rising steeply at a time when food shortage and dire poverty are the lot of the great majority of humanity. It will be a difficult matter, demanding great effort and sacrifice on the part of the better-off communities, to lift the general worldwide standard of living to a tolerable level *even if no further increase in world population takes place*. A lifting of the general standard of living will become an impossibility if the trend

---

[*] For a thoroughgoing account of the details of the problem considered in the present chapter, see Harrison Brown, *The Challenge of Man's Future,* Viking Press.

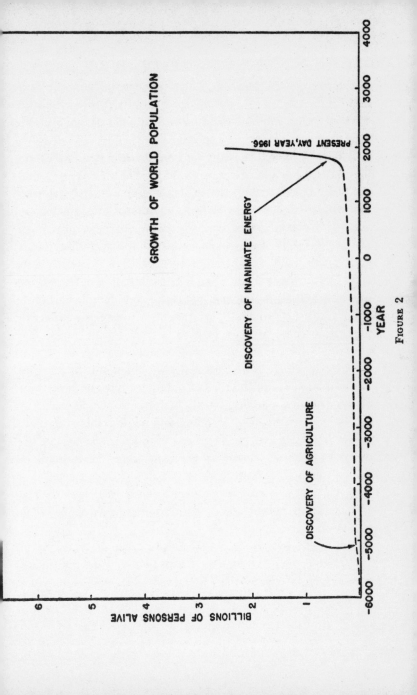

GROWTH OF WORLD POPULATION

DISCOVERY OF INANIMATE ENERGY

PRESENT DAY, YEAR 1956.

DISCOVERY OF AGRICULTURE

FIGURE 2

of the curve of Figure 2 should continue throughout the next half century. Yet a one-power world in any real sense must in the long run demand a trend toward equality of living standards.

It may be as well to point out here that the standard of living may be thought of as an "average share." Take the total production, food and otherwise, of a community and divide by the number of members of the community. The result is an average share. Of course everyone does not receive exactly an average share, some get more and some less according to circumstances. And if a community is obliged by its relations with other groups to be always in a state of preparation for war, some of the production, perhaps a considerable part of it, will be used up in making instruments of war. This applies to industrial goods only, not to food (except in rare cases). To this extent the average share may be reduced.

These remarks make it plain that production is by itself no index of standard of living. Not unless we know both the production of a community and the number of people in it, can we judge what the living standard will be. It is therefore quite useless to make plans for increasing production throughout the world unless we consider at the same time the number of people that will require to share the production. Indeed it is clear that unless the rise of production keeps pace with the rise of population there can be no improvement at all in living standards.

In the last two or three centuries production, especially of industrial goods, has increased among a few favored communities more rapidly than population—in spite of the very great rise of the latter. There has been a very good reason for this; namely the tapping by Man of the inanimate energy latent in our supplies of coal and oil. It is important to realize that our good fortune in this respect is an exceptional experience. The same good fortune has not been world-wide: it has been confined to a few communities only—essentially Europe and North America. It is also important to realize that population levels in the favored communities have already been raised to values that are commensurate with the new situation. We have had our rise of population. The increase in the number of people made possible by the unlocking of inanimate energy has already taken place. Not much more margin remains in even the most favored groups.

It has often been said that when the use of inanimate energy becomes world-wide a general global lift of living standards will occur; and that this happy state of affairs will be accompanied by a steep decline of the birth rate in the at present underdeveloped countries, a decline that will bring the world's population to stability, that will level off the steep rise of the curve of Figure 2. It would be difficult to match these statements in their absurdities. It would also be difficult to devise any other nonsense so potentially dangerous to human welfare.

In the first place the supplies of inanimate energy necessary for a world-wide industrialization are certainly not available at the present time. We are already beginning to talk about the ultimate exhaustion of oil reserves, and that in spite of the fact that oil consumption is confined to a small fraction of the world's population. If the whole world population were to consume oil at the rate that it is now being consumed in the

United States, world reserves of oil would become exhausted in not much more than thirty years. Supplies of coal are somewhat more plentiful, but not to a degree that has the slightest effect on the argument. This we can see by considering the case of Great Britain, who with only 2 per cent of the world's population possesses coal reserves that are appreciably exceeded only by the U.S., the U.S.S.R., and China. Yet Great Britain is already being troubled by the specter of coal exhaustion. Only in the case of China of all the underdeveloped lands are there sufficient resources of inanimate energy to make industrialization possible. And if the Chinese people were to consume inanimate energy on the same per capita level as the people of the United States do, the Chinese resources of coal would be exhausted in a couple of centuries or so.

The eventual answer to the problem of inanimate energy lies of course in nuclear power. We often hear about the threat to civilization of the hydrogen bomb. Let us now look at the other side of the question. Without the energy that can be released by nuclear transformations, civilization in the form that we know it and as we understand it would very likely be irretrievably doomed. Exhaustion of inanimate energy would put paid to all our ways of life; energy exhaustion would inexorably overtake us (as coal and oil supplies were used up) were it not for the development of nuclear energy. On a short-term basis nuclear power is a danger. On a long-term basis it is the salvation of mankind. Would we sooner be with it, or without it? Would you sooner live in a society faced by certain decay, or in a time of great danger and even greater opportunity?

If then nuclear power provides the way ahead, not just for a century or two but down the millennia, cannot we think of a world-wide industrialization based on nuclear power? Certainly we can, if we are willing to take the situation as it will very likely be in fifty years' time. But there can be no such world-wide industrialization today. We are still fifty years away from the time when nuclear power can take over from oil and coal. This is not to say that any doubts exist about the possibility of developing nuclear power. The basic scientific problems have already been solved, so that we can be quite clear about this. The fifty-years margin is largely a question of economics. The smooth transition from a society based on coal and oil to one based on nuclear power requires time—a fair estimate is that it will require fifty years. The time might be shortened if we were willing to accept a serious disturbance of the economic conditions, i.e., if we were willing to pay much more for nuclear energy than we are paying for the energy we use at the present time.

It follows that nuclear power does not provide an immediate solution to the problems of world-wide industrialization, although in the long run it will probably do so. But we are not really concerned now with the long run. In the short run a prolongation of the population rise shown in Figure 2 would give rise to a disastrous situation. If this curve continues for only another fifty years, mankind will be faced by an unparalleled disaster. So much then for the industrialization part of the argument.

A second fallacy is that industrialization does not guarantee any marked increase of food production. Why should it? The plant yield from a piece of land depends on the soil constituents and on sun and rain. So long as the land is adequately plowed it scarcely affects the situation whether the plow is pulled by tractors or by oxen. Likewise the yield is scarcely affected by whether reaping is done by a mechanical instrument or by a man with a scythe. It is true that artificial fertilizers are an industrial product and that their use for augmenting the natural soil constituents may have some effect on plant growth, but this is not a major point.

What then, we may ask, is the importance of industrialism to agriculture? The answer has already been indicated in an earlier chapter. Although the land may not yield significantly more under conditions of modern mechanical farming than it used to when only primitive methods were available the number of people required on the land is enormously affected by farming technique. Far fewer land workers are required when mechanical methods are used. We spoke at an earlier stage of food profits. By this we meant the excess food available over and above what is required to sustain the farm workers themselves. In primitive farming food profits are low. In "industrial" farming food profits are high, as indeed they must be in order to support the industrial communities that provided the mechanical equipment used by the farmer and the luxuries enjoyed by him.

When we take these considerations together with the population problem implied by Figure 2 several important points stand out. Although food profits in industrialized agriculture are large they are not inexhaustible. Indeed the food profits are only large because many people who would be required to work on the land under nonindustrial conditions can be dispensed with (so far as food production is concerned) and can therefore hie themselves off to the cities. Evidently an industrialized community will run into difficulties if the city population should swell to such proportions that the food profits are swallowed up. The community will then be critically dependent on outside trade, on the exchange abroad of manufactured goods for food. If food is readily available, as was the case for Britain during the nineteenth century, then the community will be able to keep the wolf from the door. But in a time of increasing world-wide food shortage the plight of such an overpopulated industrial people must become severe, as indeed it is becoming today for Britain.

The balance between farmers and industrial population is a problem that no nation seems to have solved satisfactorily. The cases of Britain, the U.S., and the U.S.S.R. all present unsatisfactory features, albeit the details differ considerably from one country to another. In Britain and the U.S. the balance has been highly unstable. When ample food has been produced, more than enough to feed the people, the farmers, instead of being appropriately rewarded for their bounty, have been offered such miserable prices that they have been brought near to beggary. When on the other hand populations have risen to such levels that farmers can barely manage to feed the people then high prices have been offered and the countryfolk have prospered exceedingly. In other words whenever conditions should have been propitious for the whole community—when there was ample for everyone—the farmers have been forced into bankruptcy; whenever conditions have become a serious threat to the survival of the community, farmers have done well. Between these two extremes of absurdity there lies only the narrowest slice of sense. Occasionally for a time a fine balance has been reached in which the food supply was adequate but not too plentiful. But such a balance is surely unstable, as unstable as a pencil balanced on its point. Let there be a rise of population in accordance with the trend of Figure 2 and the balance is destroyed, and the community is plunged into dire circumstances.

Evidently in Western civilization the relation between agriculture and industry is wrongly balanced. Farmers should be magnificently rewarded when ample food is available, not the reverse way round. The margin of stability is then tipped correctly toward a sufficiency of food. Britain today is paying the penalty for adopting this erroneous policy. Unless the United States changes its policy and controls the present rapid rise of the American population it is not merely likely but certain that she will be paying the same penalty in fifty years' time, and paying it more bitterly since there is nowhere in the world from which the United States can purchase supplies of food large enough to be of real consequence (as Britain with a smaller number of mouths to feed is still able in some measure to do). Yet in spite of this obvious danger some American politicians in high places have actually told farmers that the rise of population is to be welcomed since it will ensure the maintenance of high prices. It will. Food is apt to become very expensive when everybody is hungry.

The situation in Russia is different but no more satisfactory. The industrial population in Russia instead of attempting to reach any accommodation with the farmers adopted a policy of wholesale brigandage. Supported by the guns and pistols manufactured in the towns the industrial population (styling themselves as Bolsheviks) threw the farmers off the land. Then not knowing themselves how to farm, these city people forced the farmers to till the very land from which they had been evicted, the farms then being styled "collective." This policy has borne the fruit that it deserves. Food production has increased hardly at all in Russia during the last forty years, perhaps by 4 or 5 per cent but no more. Whether the Russian farm laborers understand the situation in any analytical sense is to be doubted, but in an instinctive way they have developed a sullen distrust of Soviet politicians. Communism apparently has little tangible success with the agricultural population of Russia.

Let us turn now to the at present nonindustrialized countries and to the nonsensical suggestion that miraculous increases in their food production will be forthcoming from industrialization. The manifest failure of the European and American industrial societies to achieve a satisfactory stable relationship with their own farming people is itself a warning of danger, quite apart from a further serious contradiction. Countries such as China are already cultivated nearly to a maximum. Consequently industrialization cannot possibly achieve any decisive increase of food production. The industrialization of China, if it could be achieved, would free a very large number of men who now work on the land. These men would be available to do other things—to build roads, to make automobiles, and so forth. But unless China could

K

send her industrial goods abroad in exchange for food, as Britain does at present, this would be small comfort to a hungry population. We can scarcely imagine that the exchange of industrial goods for food is something that every nation can do. So long as industrial goods were scarce, as they were in the nineteenth century, the British exchange policy was a workable one. As time has gone on, the spread of industrialization has decreased the world-wide demand for manufactured articles, and industrialization of the backward countries will complete this trend. Simultaneously, rising populations throughout the world are decreasing the number of communities with an exportable food surplus. Soon every nation will be wanting to exchange manufactures that nobody wants for food that no one has got. We cannot expect therefore that the industrialization of the Far East (enormous job that it would be) will offer the slightest possibility of feeding the rapidly increasing, ill-nourished, oriental populations. The much more likely effect of such an industrialization would be to plunge the world into a disastrous holocaust. When we consider how much trouble the so-far industrialized countries have got themselves into, and that the people of these countries comprise only a small proportion of the world's total population (U.S., U.S.S.R., Germany, and Britain have effectively the whole world's industrialization with only 20 per cent of the world's population) I think we may shiver to contemplate what might happen in a wholly industrialized world populated by starving billions.

The best hope of increasing the world's food supply lies in projects that could be operated by the at present industrialized countries, not at all by the further spread of industrialism into already densely populated underdeveloped areas. Industrialization allows marginal lands to be brought under cultivation, lands that could not be cultivated under agrarian conditions because the number of manual workers required would be so great that the food grown would be insufficient to feed them. Such territory is "uneconomic" under agrarian conditions in a deep sense of the word. But with the mechanical methods provided by industrialism, food profits might be shown.

The most notable areas of marginal lands lie in the tropics —Africa and South America—and in the semi-Arctic—Siberia and Northern Canada. It has been estimated that if all these lands could be brought under cultivation world food production might be increased by some 70 or 80 per cent.

Accepting this perhaps somewhat optimistic view of the situation some people have argued that here is a solution of the population problem. Such a view is quite erroneous. In the first place the adequate nourishment of the present population of the world, without allowing for any further increase of numbers, requires a substantial increase of food production. Much of the increase that can be got by bringing tropical and semi-Arctic soils under cultivation should go into improving the diet of people now alive, and is therefore not to be considered as available for providing for a greater number of people—if we take at all seriously the often repeated desire both of the Anti-Communists and of the Communist camps to raise the condition of the bulk of humanity above starvation level. Certainly it is hardly to be expected that we shall have a world at peace until this is done.

But quite apart from this present demand for more food, a

continuation of the rise shown in Figure 2 would in time swallow up the increased production from the marginal lands. Even if we grant the optimistic assessment of the potentialities of these lands, their productivity will enable the availability of food to keep pace with the rising world population for only another fifty years or so, and that is a triflingly short time compared with the ancestry of our civilization. So much then for one of the absurdities that are constantly being served up by economists, politicians, and Catholic religious leaders as a solution of the world population problem.

Let us follow the optimists a little further. They say that Man's ingenuity will think up new methods and ideas as the necessity arises. When in fifty years' time the productivity of the marginal lands becomes a vital necessity to support, at starvation level, a world population of 4,000 millions, new agricultural methods will be invented that will support at starvation level a still greater number. Let us follow the optimists in this. It is indeed already known that a substantial rise in nutritive values might be achieved if the plants now cultivated by farmers were replaced by algae. The algae are single-celled plants that grow in ponds, lakes, and in the sea. A watery habitat is necessary for their growth, so that the replacement of present agriculture by what we may term algaeculture would require much of the land surface to be converted into a huge shallow pond. But let us be optimistic and suppose that this is done, that a large part of North America, Europe, and Asia is awash with algaè farms. Then food production might be increased in nutritive value about fivefold. This would allow

20,000 million people to live at starvation level, a situation that will be reached—the curve of Figure 2 continuing to rise —in about two hundred years.

A lease of two hundred years of life gives the optimists ample scope for imagination. In two hundred years it should be possible, they argue, to dream up all sorts of devices—quite apart from swilling the whole Earth with water. It might be possible for instance to produce food synthetically. At one end of a factory simple chemicals will be fed in—carbon dioxide, water, nitrogen, phosphates—and will then be processed into the proteins, fats, and carbohydrates required by our bodies. So we pass from algaeculture to pillculture. In this way it is argued that food effectively without limit may be made available.

I am sorry to disillusion the optimists. Their wonderful ideas must come to nought for an unfortunate practical reason. In about eleven hundred years the amount of standing room on the Earth will become insufficient. Today we talk of a nation having an average of so-many-persons-to-the-square-mile. Eleven hundred years hence this will seem a fantastically spacious situation, for in eleven hundred years the entire land surface will be covered with people, one person to every square yard—including mountains and deserts too.

When this stage is reached it will be necessary either to cover the whole land surface with skyscrapers or for humanity to follow the mole and to live underground. By so doing it will be possible for people to live one over the other. This further ingenuity will be good for quite a long time, always provided it proves possible to refrigerate the interior of the Earth which unrefrigerated is far too hot a place for the likes of us. Optimism in the field of gigantic refrigerators will give us another four thousand years, making a total future of just over five thousand years, nearly as long into the future as the civilization of Mesopotamia lies into the past. The reason for this new limit is again a practical one. After a little more than five thousand years the bulk of humanity will be so vast that its total weight, all persons added together, will exceed the Earth itself. This means that we shall run out of space inside the Earth. Ingenious termites, living always on synthetic pills, we shall be crowded out, not only horizontally, but vertically as well.

At this stage, if not before, we must evidently leave the Earth and undertake the job of populating the Universe. I do not mean just the planets attached to our own Sun, but the myriads of planets that are probably to be found in the vicinity of other stars. Vast numbers of us will then hie ourselves off into the depths of space, which will probably seem quite a pleasant experience after several thousand years of squeezing at the Earth's center where the pressure amounts to some twenty million pounds per square inch.

Again we can expect a new lease of life, but not for an indefinite time I am sorry to say. After a further six thousand years the total mass of humanity will exceed the mass of the whole visible Universe, all the visible stars and galaxies. And here I refuse to follow the ingenious optimists any further. Algaeculture, yes; pillculture, yes; one person to the square yard, yes; refrigerate the Earth, yes; populate the Universe, yes; but exceed the Universe, no.

To speak seriously, the estimates I have just given are all impeccably correct *if* we assume that the curve of Figure 2 continues to climb with the same slope that it has at the present time. The absurdity of our results is a certain indication that the world's population will not go on indefinitely increasing at its present rate. The slope of the population curve must tail off in some such fashion as I have indicated in Figure 3. The word *must* is unqualified. Our optimistic nonsensicalities show that it must.

Granted this unassailable conclusion we can now pass to a stringent question. What processes will operate to force the population curve to round itself off? Two quite different answers can be suggested. One is that the human population will ultimately be limited by famine and war, much as the numbers of other animal species are limited. The second possibility is that we shall perceive the grim shadow of world starvation ahead of us and voluntarily limit our population in the nick of time. One or other of these answers must prove correct. So much is certain. It does not lie in our choice. What does lie in our choice is which answer will prove correct. Do we wish to be limited forcibly as the beasts of the fields and forests are, or do we wish to maintain our present ways of life, our pursuit of the arts and of knowledge, our civilization?

Nothing much more remains to be said on this subject. The choice is a stark one and it must be made whether we like it or not. It only remains to say a few words about the optimists. The most notorious optimists belong to two groups that are

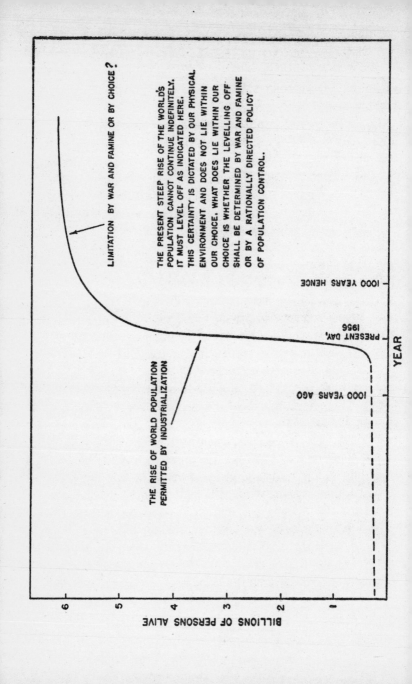

LIMITATION BY WAR AND FAMINE OR BY CHOICE?

THE PRESENT STEEP RISE OF THE WORLD'S
POPULATION CANNOT CONTINUE INDEFINITELY.
IT MUST LEVEL OFF AS INDICATED HERE.
THIS CERTAINTY IS DICTATED BY OUR PHYSICAL
ENVIRONMENT AND DOES NOT LIE WITHIN
OUR CHOICE. WHAT DOES LIE WITHIN OUR
CHOICE IS WHETHER THE LEVELLING OFF
SHALL BE DETERMINED BY WAR AND FAMINE
OR BY A RATIONALLY DIRECTED POLICY
OF POPULATION CONTROL.

THE RISE OF WORLD POPULATION
PERMITTED BY INDUSTRIALIZATION

YEAR

1000 YEARS HENCE

PRESENT DAY, 1956

1000 YEARS AGO

BILLIONS OF PERSONS ALIVE

6
5
4
3
2
1

opposed to each other in all other matters except on this population problem. They are the Communists and the Roman Catholics—at first sight strange bedfellows, but not so strange when one ponders more deeply. Both Catholic and Communists argue by dogma. An argument is judged "right" by these people because they judge it to be based on "right" premises, not because it leads to results that accord with the facts. Indeed if the facts of the case should disagree with the dogma then so much the worse for the facts.

In part by this wrongheadedness and in part through flagrant dishonesty the Communists and Catholics arrive at a co-point of view on the population question. Effective steps toward a voluntary limitation of families is forbidden to Catholics because by so doing the proportion of Catholics to non-Catholics tends to be steadily increased. The Communists for their part are cravenly afraid to face up to the population issue because of the loss of prestige that they might suffer in the great Asiatic countries. Communist policy seeks to infiltrate into the Far East by ascribing the low oriental standard of life to Western inefficiency and exploitation. To admit that the low standard arises from too high populations, and that the standard will go still lower as populations continue to rise, would destroy this communist policy.

Thus it seems that both Communists and Catholics are determined to plunge the world into further misery, both for what are essentially the same end—an increase of their own power. The practical difficulty of dealing with the population problem as we have discussed it above is enormously increased by this miserable attitude. It seems well-nigh certain that in the years to come, if these people have their way, untold multitudes will be reduced to extreme privation. Potentially great men, potential Beethovens, potential Newtons, potential Shakespeares will be broken by a lack of sustenance in a poverty-stricken world.

XIII.

Fossilization: The Third Problem

IT MAY seem somewhat surprising that the problems of the last two chapters appear in some respects less severe than a third problem that must confront the world should these two problems ever be solved. Less severe because the two earlier problems are clearly susceptible of solution (the problem of war by the adoption of a one-power world and the problem of economic sufficiency by a suitable policy of population control), whereas it is not clear that the third problem has any solution at all. This is the problem of fossilization. We have seen how established dominant communities tend to become fossilized. History gives us numerous examples. So far fossilization has not presented any serious problem, because in a multipower world the fossilization of a particular community simply leads to the decline, and probably to the disintegration in war, of the community in question. Its place is then taken by another more go-ahead group, which in turn becomes replaced by a further group once fossilization overtakes it. Fossilization is no serious problem in a multipower war-racked world. But it must become a serious problem in a single-power world without war.

There may be some who will say, "Why worry? Why should a single-power fossilized world be unpleasant to live in?" The answer, I think, is that the human individual possesses wired-in qualities of courage and enterprise that contradict fossilization, and that these wired-in qualities must cause serious widespread frustration in a fossilized world. As an Englishman I myself have some conception of what would be implied in such a situation. British society today is partially fossilized. As a simple almost trivial example, take the British monetary system. Everyone agrees that it would be an advantage to have a decimal monetary system, as the United States has. Everyone agrees that the British penny is absurdly bulky in relation to its value. Both these disadvantages can be overcome, as a friend has pointed out, by a simple revaluation of the penny, a procedure that would cause no serious economic repercussions. Instead of the present valuation of twelve pence to the shilling, the valuation should be five pence to the shilling. We then have the following situation:

1 pound sterling = 20 shillings = 10 "two-shillings"
1 "two-shillings" = 10 pence

Since the British already have a coin for "two-shillings," a decimal system lies immediately to hand. Not only this, but a penny would then become a far more useful coin, being of a correct value for local postage stamps, local telephone calls, newspapers, etc. I mention all this in detail because here we have a case where a very simple, quite easily carried out change would be a great advantage. Yet it is completely impossible (so it seems) to get this change made.

Another simple advantageous idea, applicable this time also to the United States, may be mentioned. This is a change in the method of voting in elections. Instead of only counting positive votes, it should be possible to cast negative votes. Instead of being obliged to cast a positive vote for one of a number of candidates, all of whom you may regard as unsatisfactory, it should be possible for you to cast a negative vote against any one candidate to whom you take the strongest exception. The candidate elected would be the candidate with the highest positive score, or more probably the least negative score. The advantage of this system of voting is that it would in a large measure break the stranglehold of the big party juggernauts and give a reasonable fighting chance to the capable independent candidate. By common consent our democracies are suffering very seriously from lack of independent thinkers among our political representatives. Instead of being genuine democracies, Britain and the United States are in effect regimes with two very nearly identical alternatives. Nazi Germany and Fascist Italy were, and Communist Russia is, a totalitarian regime with only one possibility. The democratic West deprecates such systems of government. But is it really a great deal better to have only a choice between near identities? You are given a choice of Republican or Democrat. But suppose you don't want either? What then?

Actually, our system is a considerable improvement on complete totalitarianism. It is always possible to write to a Republican representative saying that you dislike the way he is voting in Congress, and to say that unless he mends his ways you will cast your vote for his Democratic opponent at the next election (or of course vice versa). In this way it is possible for the people of the United States to put pressure on their political representatives. But the pressure is of a negative unsatisfactory sort, not to be compared with being able to vote for the man you really want.

Now why does a scheme of positive and negative votes give a very much better chance of election to a capable independent candidate? Because a capable respected man would attract very few negative votes, while candidates sheltering under the party machines would probably attract as many negative votes as positive. A man, Mr. A, who at present votes for Mr. X, Democrat, is probably as much concerned to *keep out* Mr. Y, Republican, as he is to get in Mr. X. Under my system the present voting:

Mr. X, Democrat, 1
Mr. Y, Republican, 0
Mr. Z, Independent, 0

might well be changed to:

Mr. X, Democrat, 0
Mr. Y, Republican, —1
Mr. Z, Independent, 0

Another voter, Mr. B, of different political persuasion is much exercised in his mind to keep out the Democratic candidate. Mr. B's voting at present is:

Mr. X, Democrat, 0
Mr. Y, Republican, 1
Mr. Z, Independent, 0

but according to my system it would become:

Mr. X, Democrat, —1
Mr. Y, Republican, 0
Mr. Z, Independent, 0

The effect of the votes of Messrs. A and B under the present system is to put Mr. Z one vote behind both the other two candidates. But under my system, Mr. Z might well emerge one vote ahead of each of his rivals. Evidently the difference is considerable and the change is to the advantage of the capable, responsible, independent candidate, who by common consent is very much needed to refresh our at present somewhat jaded party-machine-dominated democratic institutions. Yet our communities are I believe much too fossilized to contemplate making such a simple adjustment in electoral procedure.

And if we have such clear evidence of fossilization in the present-day world, constantly stirred up by intercommunity rivalries, how much more rigid might a single-power world become? Wherein lies the solution? I must say frankly that I do not know. It is possible to make suggestions as to how the problem might be tackled, but whether the suggestions would prove adequate seems quite uncertain.

The first point I would stress as important is that more attention should be given to the relation of the individual to the whole aggregate of humanity. Those who have been primarily concerned with ethical and moral issues seem to me to have systematically undervalued the importance of the structural organization of humanity as a whole. This is I think in a large measure the outcome of the doctrines of the Christian Churches which have almost exclusively been concerned with the relationship of the individual to his neighbors. Such a relationship is undoubtedly important, and in bringing about the satisfactory neighborly relations that exist today in Western society the Churches have certainly done an excellent job. Where I cannot agree with them, however, is in their claim that proper neighborly behavior is enough. It is not axiomatic, and indeed I think it to be an entire fallacy, to suppose that if every individual behaves reasonably toward his immediate neighbors then society as a whole will get along too. Humanity as a whole is a living organism with properties that are not readily perceived by a consideration of individual components. I have sought to stress this very point in earlier chapters by referring to this large-scale organism as The Thing. It is high time that more study was devoted to the properties of The Thing. In this way it may eventually be possible to gain a far greater understanding of human affairs than we possess at present, and with understanding may come the measure of control that we are now so manifestly lacking. In the meantime some helpful things can be said.

While it is certain that a clash between the interests of the individual and The Thing is more than likely to end in the victory of The Thing, it is important to realize that many features of our social organizations are of indifferent interest to The Thing. In such matters we possess a genuine freedom of choice, and there is no reason why the choice should not take such a form as to secure maximum concessions to the individual.

An example may be of interest. We have seen that a clash exists between The Thing and our present desire to build a multipower world. The Thing demands a single-power world, and I think that whatever we do as individuals and whatever we want, it will be a single-power world that we shall ultimately get. But a single-power world is not the same thing as a world of cultural uniformity. In the Swiss Confederation the different cantons act together for purposes of defense and national finance, but they differ greatly in their internal domestic organizations and even in their languages. In a like manner we can imagine a single-power world in the economic and military sense, but not in the cultural sense. There seems no reason why a culturally diversified world should not persist, and why cultural differences should not play a big part in the avoidance of international fossilization.

In short it is important that in the future we should separate clearly those things that we must do from those that we need not do. The necessity for a single-power world is overriding but the necessity for a world of conformity is not. The more picturesque differences of custom the better, even within what we regard today as a single nation.

Also in this connection it is important to realize that a perfect state of society is a chimera. A man dreams of Utopia when he finds serious inconsistencies in the practices of the society in which he happens to live. Utopia to him is a society in most respects similar to his own, but with all the inconsistencies removed. The pleasurable quality of Utopia lies, of course, in this removal of inconsistency.

Now some people have questioned whether Utopia, if indeed it could be sampled, would turn out to be as desirable a place as is generally supposed. Once the first pleasurable flush had worn off, what then? To answer this question we need only notice that in an entirely static society monotony must soon ensue, while in a changing society new inconsistencies must tend to arise sooner or later. Thus even if we could set up Utopia at the present time, we should have no guarantee that our society would continue to be Utopian for any great length of time. Small inconsistencies would soon develop, and unless corrected, would grow gradually into large inconsistencies, so that eventually things would become as bad as before. The proviso "unless corrected" is most important here, for we now see that it is not enough for mankind to make one all-out effort to set itself to rights; mankind must endlessly go on making the effort to keep itself right. An enormous spasmodic effort might perhaps set up a modern Utopia, but we should need to exert ourselves continuously to maintain it.

It may be useful to consider an analogy. Let us suppose an airplane is flying around somewhere in the sky and that our job is to locate it with a searchlight. We have the awkward task of first getting the plane in the beam; this is equivalent to setting up Utopia. Then follows the problem of preventing the plane from jinking out of the light; this corresponds to maintaining the Utopian society. The best way of actually keeping a searchlight locked on to an aircraft is by the use of a box of tricks known as a feedback mechanism. As soon as the aircraft tries to fly out of the light, the feedback mechanism takes note of what is happening, and then passes instructions to the searchlight telling it just what movement is required to bring the center of the beam back on to the plane again.

Actually we are using feedback systems every minute of the day without realizing it. We use a feedback system far more complicated than the automatic searchlight every time we stretch out a hand to pick up some object. The eye supplies information to the brain about the position of the object and about the position of the hand. The muscles supply information about the motion of the hand. From this the brain calculates by how much the hand is going to miss the object if it persists in its present motion. A further calculation is next performed to decide how the muscles should be altered in order to bring the hand nearer to the object. The result of this calculation is then transmitted as a direction to the muscles. By frequent repetition of this procedure the hand is finally brought into contact with the object. The whole process happens very quickly so that normally we pay little attention to it. Its working can, however, be observed in slow motion, as it were, by watching a baby of eight or nine months trying to pick up a crumb.

These examples bring out the essential feature of a feedback control system. Accuracy is maintained, not by a rigid prevention of errors, but through their immediate correction should they arise. The very existence of the error produces its own correction. Thus as soon as the aircraft tends to fly out of the searchlight beam the very action of the aircraft itself has the effect of causing the searchlight to pick it up again.

Now to return to our Utopian society. A truly Utopian society would be one, not as usually imagined with impossible static perfection, but one endowed with the property of a feedback control mechanism. Temporary perfection is not so important as a procedure for removing inconsistencies as soon as they arise; a procedure whereby an inconsistency itself sets in operation the means for its own correction.

XIV.

The Religious Impulse in Man

LANGUAGE is a phenomenally clever medium for expressing the activity that goes on in our brains, the activity that we describe as "thinking." Words are labels that we attach to concepts and ideas. When we speak or write we show the labels corresponding to our "thoughts" to each other. Yet ingenious and indispensable as the processes of language are, no one who has tried to express himself precisely (as we say) can remain unaware of the difficulties and shortcomings of language. The play of our thoughts cannot be communicated to others in their full vividness. All we can do is to hold up to each other a set of labels which may or may not be suitably matched to our ideas. One of the difficulties of putting a new idea across is that in its nature a new idea may be indescribable in terms of old labels. New labels, new words, have to be invented and have to be conveyed successfully to others. Almost always the delay in the acceptance of a new idea comes from the delay in the invention of suitable new labels and in their promulgation. Often enough an idea that seems utterly obscure to one generation seems quite obvious to the next generation. The reason is that suitable new labels have had time to become widely diffused. It is in this matter of the labeling of ideas that the real Babel lies, not in differences of language. Languages differ only in the sense that the labels are associated with different sounds, not in the system of labeling. Notice how quickly it happens that when a new label has been invented in one language, essentially the same label spreads into other languages.

There is perhaps no section of human affairs in which this matter of labeling causes the confusion that it does in discussions of religion. Even the meaning that we attach to the word "religion" is open to misunderstandings, disagreements, and confusion. The same may be said of a host of other labels "God," "faith," "material," "spiritual," "blasphemy," and so on. What I propose to do in this chapter is to try to indicate what I mean when I use these labels.

Much of the difficulty in discussing religious questions arises from the penchant of those who claim to be religious for displacing a question. Consider the following sequence of questions and answers.

Q. What does religion consist of?
A. A belief in the power of God.
Q. What is God?
A. The eternal, the almighty.
Q. What is "eternal," what is "almighty"?

At each stage here the questioner is asking for an explanation of the concept underlying a particular label, and by way of answer he only receives other equally unintelligible labels. It seems to me that this sort of discussion gets one nowhere at all.

Religion if it has any sensible meaning does not consist, or more properly should not consist, in holding beliefs by "faith" that are denied by rational thought. For instance I do not regard a belief that Jesus was born of a virgin as evidence of a religious turn of mind. A denial of rational thought in favor of beliefs of this sort that contradict the very fabric of the world is to negate the faculty that separates Man from the beasts of the fields and forests. Religion, if it is not to be pernicious nonsense, must be based on rational thinking.

Instead of considering religion by way of conventional beliefs let us approach the subject from an unexpected direction. In the last three chapters we have discussed three problems, each of great importance to mankind. There remains a fourth problem, perhaps still more important and certainly more difficult than the other three. This we may call the "problem of purpose." Imagine that you have all the things that you would like, and that you have achieved all your ambitions. What then? A very dull life indeed. The word "happiness" is one of the most difficult of all labels. Certainly happiness does not lie in a state of dreamy contemplation, it is not Nirvana. Happiness is a dynamic state of mind, associated with the active fulfillment of our desires. Once fulfillment is over happiness is lost. A man with a vast fortune often attains all his ambitions and wants, thereby using up his store of happiness. He becomes blasé and sophisticated, to use two more labels. It is clear then that an "end" in life, or better still many such "ends," are important to the individual.

By and large this matter of "end" and "purpose" is most frequently satisfied in the rearing of a family; especially is it so in the case of women. But there are many other "aims" that a man or woman can have—success in a career, the solving of a scientific problem, achievement in one or other of the arts, playing a musical instrument, writing a book, climbing a mountain. It is the possession of one or several of these aims by the majority of individuals that keeps our modern communities in a more or less sane condition.

Yet this is not all. The sense of purpose in the life of an individual seems incomplete unless the whole community in which he lives possesses a common sense of purpose. A community with a clear-cut aim will be an enthusiastic, lively body —and if the aim should be achieved, for a time a happy body. Stagnation, fossilization, produces the contrary effect, leaving the individual with a sense of frustration, even if he should himself be possessed of an adequate stock of personal ambitions.

Today the communist countries are the ones with the clearest aims. Both Russia and China, the latter particularly, are backward economically and have a great deal of leeway to make up before the condition of their peoples becomes comparable with that of the Western countries. It is the sense of purpose arising from a tackling of their economic problems that gives the communists their ebullient confidence. The champagne-like quality of their sense of national purpose is so strong that the Chinese and Russian people have been willing to give up a large measure of personal liberty in order to achieve it. This would be all very well if the communists did not go on to conclude in their enthusiasm that what may possibly be good for them is good for the rest of the world. This is not so. The United States is not backward economically and the American people do not need to give up any personal liberties.

The present enthusiasm of Russia and China cannot in any case be permanent. It represents an expansion phase no different in its economic roots to the U.S. expansion of the nineteeth and early twentieth centuries, no different indeed from the expansion phases of a hundred and one communities that can be traced in the historical record. We have mentioned several times the expansion phase that precedes fossilization. Such expansions are in their nature temporary and therefore do not supply humanity with a permanent sense of purpose.

A similar situation applies I think to the three problems discussed in the last three chapters. Here we have problems that can very well give us a sense of purpose, but of a temporary nature only. Once the problems of population, of fossilization, and of the single-power world have been conquered, humanity will be very much like the wealthy individual bored with life because he has gratified all his whims. What then? Where does the ultimate purpose, or aim if you like, of the human species lie? What is the point of the species reproducing itself generation by generation? Why are we journeying? It is in the propounding of questions such as these, and in attempting to answer them that (I would say) the religious impulse lies.

There are no easy answers to these questions, as is clear from the multitude of contradictory religious beliefs that have been held in the world. Yet an examination of the origins of the major religions will show that in spite of contradictions their tenets spring from a common aim: the identification of Man with the Universe. To be sure this aim is a little difficult to discover in contemporary religions. There is a reason for this. Contemporary religion is based on the religious teachings of bygone eras, often teachings that are very much older than the adherents of the modern religions realize, so old indeed that they belong to days when men understood comparatively little either about themselves or about the Universe. It was natural therefore that serious mistakes were made, mistakes that cannot survive a modern scrutiny by the rationally minded. But instead of recognizing this, contemporary religion has preferred to stick to the letter, rather than to the spirit, of the old beliefs. Faced then with outrageous contradictions it has become necessary to be increasingly vague about the meanings of the labels that describe the religious concepts—a point that we have already noted. It is to be doubted whether the situation can be retrieved by an attempt to clarify the present confused situation. Rather does it seem far more profitable to attempt to rebuild our ideas of Man's relation to the Universe from a new start, putting aside the older beliefs until some rational basis for discussing them has been achieved.

What then can we say of Man's relation to the Universe? Do we know that there is any relation at all, except that Man is some curious by-product of the Universe? Yes, I think we do know something rather surprising on this point. A digression on science and scientific discovery is necessary to make this clear.

To most people the success that has been achieved by science seems truly remarkable. Take for instance the ability of the Newtonian theory of gravitation to predict several years ahead just when and where an eclipse of the Sun is going to occur. Or again, consider a remarkable outcome of Maxwell's theory of light: this theory correctly predicted all the properties of radio, long before the existence of radio was discovered experimentally. Einstein's theory correctly predicted that light passing near the Sun would be deflected in its path. Dirac's theory of the electron correctly predicted the existence of a new type of particle, the positron. Many other examples of a like nature could be given.

Now what is so striking about all these cases is the way in which it was found possible to describe a vast range of physical phenomena in terms of a quite small number of mathematical equations. Not only this, but in each of the cases just mentioned, first a group of physical phenomena was discovered experimentally, second it was found that the observations could be completely represented by mathematical equations, third the mathematical equations turned out to have wider implications than the original observations on which they were based, and fourth these wider implications were used with complete success to predict new phenomena not known to exist up to then, and indeed not even suspected to exist. It is no exaggeration to describe this correspondence between observations and mathematics as completely astounding. The element of mystery in it never wears off, no matter how familiar we may become with the details. We cease to wonder at an ordinary conjuring trick once we know how it is done. In contrast, the more we know of how the scientific conjuring trick is done, the more we continue to be amazed by it.

This astonishing ability of the human brain to guess the workings of the Universe seems explicable only on the basis that in some degree at least our brains mirror the Universe itself. As Lyttleton has said, it looks as though we carry the pattern of the Universe about inside our own heads. Even on the most cautious view the connection must be reckoned a most remarkable one.

Christians say that Man was created in the image of God. Provided we make the association

God = The Universe

the Christian statement becomes very much what we have just been saying. I feel sure that many religious people would object to this association, however, but what would they offer in its place? What concept does the label "God" stand for? Some people would seem to think of "God" as the "maker" of the Universe. The concept here would seem to be analogous to that of a man-made machine, the role of "God" as "He watches" the Universe from "outside" being analogous to that of a girl tending a spinning wheel. Indeed according to Catholics "God" did such a poor job in his "making" of the Universe that it is constantly necessary for "Him" to be making adjustments ("miracles") when things go wrong, rather as the girl may have to keep adjusting her spinning wheel. Ironically it is just those people who hold this flagrant machine concept who refer to themselves as "spiritually minded" and who castigate rational opinions. I would urge most strongly that the notion of something (undefined) "outside" the Universe should be dropped from all our ways of thinking, and that if we wish to use the label "God" it should be used only in the above association of concepts. The Universe constitutes everything that there is.

It is worth adding a few words on incorrect uses of such labels as "matter," "materialistic," "spiritual," and the like. In the old days when very little was known about matter it seemed as if the difference between an inert body (such as a stone) and an active body (such as a human) could only be explained on the basis that the active body possessed some "vitalizing agent" which the stone did not. Thus the following associations became current:

stone = matter

human = matter + vitalizing agent

the vitalizing agent being described as "spiritual," and being referred to as the "soul."

Nowadays knowing a great deal more about matter we would rewrite the identities in the following way

stone = matter organized in a simple way

human = matter in a highly complex organization

In a sense the former duality is still preserved, with the highly complex human organization taking the place of the vitalizing agent. In a sense it is correct to think of the organization as something separate from the matter. It is well known that the actual matter of which a man is made up changes with time. That is to say the identity of the atoms in a man's body changes. But this does not necessarily produce any change in the man, because the change in the atoms need not cause any change in the organization—one molecule of water can replace another, one atom of phosphorus can replace another, and so on. There is nothing unduly remarkable about all this. The building of a house is not simply a matter of ordering a pile of building materials. A structural design is also required. Indeed when a person builds a house the first thing to engage attention is the plan, the organization. A house is a collection of materials plus an organization. The distinction will be abundantly clear not only to those who have built a house, but also to those who have had a house destroyed—as many did during the late war.

In accordance with these ideas we can give meanings to such labels as "soul," "spiritual," and so on. These are concepts that relate to the organization, not to the particular materials that constitute a person. Your "personality" is determined by your organization, the difference between one person and another is a difference of organization

"You" = "Your organization"

"Me" = "My organization"

"Jack Smith" = "The organized structure of Jack Smith."

Perhaps I can make this clearer by an idealized experiment. Suppose I take you to pieces, disintegrate you into atoms. Then "You" will cease to exist, "You" will cease to feel, your "Soul" will have been destroyed, the organization will have gone. But suppose that before I disintegrate you I take a careful record (supposing this to be possible) of how all the atoms of your body are fitted together. In short I prepare a blueprint of the organization which is "You." Let us suppose further that this blueprint survives for many centuries and eventually, say a thousand years hence, comes into the hands of a man who is clever enough to put atoms of matter (of which there are always plenty on hand) back into their original arrangement. What would happen? "You" would come alive again, exactly and precisely as you are at the present moment.

This may not be as comforting as those who follow contemporary religions would like, but it may come as a surprise to many to realize that there is no logical finality about "death." It is true that, at present, blueprints of this sort cannot be made, nor could a blueprint, even if we had one, be used for constructional purposes. But these are failures of technique, not of principle. It may come as a surprise, even to Christians, to realize that resurrection can be placed on a logical footing. Whether it can ever be put on a practical footing is another issue, one to which we know no answer.

But the main point I wish to bring out is that considerable progress can be made toward understanding Man's relation to the Universe. This can be done without any of the ancient beliefs, and without "faith." The purely scientific approach to such issues as "life," "death," "soul," and so on already reveals more in the way of remarkable conclusions than we might have expected. The picture is not yet complete, or anything like complete. Nor should we expect it to be, since it has become clear in recent years that science itself is still only at the beginning of the road. Recent studies of the ultrasmall in nuclear physics and of the ultralarge in astronomy have made it plain that there are whole worlds of understanding still to be opened up to us. And it is scarcely to be supposed that vitally new scientific knowledge will have no relation to the subject of our present discussion. There are some always ready to assert that science is a barren study, and that only by "faith" in the efficacy of ill-understood labels can the "truth" be perceived. How it comes about that the Universe revealed by painstaking scientific investigation is so incomparably grander than anything that the "men of faith" have ever told us about, I have never yet heard tell.

We started the present chapter by saying that life will be found empty unless the continuity of the human species is endowed with a sense of purpose. We saw that aims of economic sufficiency, of national aspirations, may prove an adequate inducement for a time, but for a time only. In the long run a broader perspective is needed. Perhaps an answer can now be offered as to what this perspective might be. By continuing to search out the ways of the Universe and of Man's relation to the Universe we shall be serving our deepest instincts and we shall be following a progressive line of development. In this can lie our aim.

There is some indication that people are moving already in this direction. There is a looking outward from the Earth, a desire of Man to feel that he has a part in the great play of the Universe.

GEORGE ALLEN & UNWIN LTD
London: 40 Museum Street, W.C.1

Auckland: 24 Wyndham Street
Bombay: 15 Graham Road, Ballard Estate, Bombay 1
Calcutta: 17 Chittaranjan Avenue, Calcutta 13
Cape Town: 109 Long Street
Karachi: Methersons Estate, Wood Street, Karachi 2
New Delhi: 13-14 Ajmeri Gate Extension, New Delhi 1
São Paulo: Avenida 9 de Julho 1138-Ap. 51
Singapore, South East Asia and Far East: 36c Prinsep Street
Sydney, N.S.W.: Bradbury House, 55 York Street
Toronto: 91 Wellington Street West